I HEAR YO

The Surprisingly Simple Skill Behind
Extraordinary Relationships

MICHAEL S. SORENSEN

CONTENTS

ACKNOWLEDGMENTS

This book, and my own understanding of the principles therein, could not have come about without the wisdom and counsel of my mentor, life coach, and friend, Jodi Hildebrandt. I owe much of my understanding of healthy relationships and effective communication to her and the several years she spent guiding, teaching, and mentoring me.

I also owe much to my parents who taught by example the importance of honesty, generosity, and compassion in my daily interactions. I would not be where I am today without their patience, support, guidance, and inspiration.

INTRODUCTION

"Remember that everyone you meet is afraid
of something, loves something, and has
lost something."

– H. Jackson Brown, Jr.

"Are you from around here?"

"I grew up in California but I've lived here for the past fifteen years. You?"

I had just picked this woman up for a first date and we were headed to a local frozen yogurt shop. She'd had a long day at work and I figured I'd keep it short and casual—take a half hour, get to know her a little better, and ask her out for the weekend if all went well.

Typical small talk ensued, but I immediately felt like she didn't want to be there. It seemed like more than just disinterest—she felt closed off. She was slouched back in her chair; gave short, almost inaudible answers; and kept looking around as if searching for a clock or an excuse to leave.

When I'd first met her a week prior, she had been friendly, outgoing, and amazingly chipper. The woman sitting across from me now, though, was anything but. It didn't seem to matter what I said or what I asked her about; she made it quite obvious that she wasn't in the mood to talk.

I continued trying to keep the conversation afloat for another ten minutes or so before finally giving up. We hopped back in my car and headed back. As we drove, I asked about her family. She paused for a moment, then indicated that it was a sensitive subject. "Ah," I thought, "that might explain things." I expected her to just leave it at that, but, to my surprise, she began to open up.

"My parents are in the middle of a divorce," she said.

"Oh . . . " I replied, suddenly feeling tremendous compassion for her, "I'm *so* sorry."

"It's okay," she muttered, putting on a pretty unconvincing tough-girl face. "I'm fine."

"Uh . . . no? Having your parents divorce isn't 'fine,'" I said. "That's got to be *incredibly* hard."

"Yeah, it actually really sucks," she quickly confirmed, letting go of her façade.

"And then on top of it, I just found out that my dad is getting married to another woman and I'm not even invited to the wedding. They just separated like a month ago!" she said.

"Are you serious?"

"Yeah. It sucks. He sends money occasionally but it just feels like a slap in the face, like he thinks money will fix everything. Like he thinks he can just move on and leave me and my mom behind. And then suddenly I hear that he's getting married in Hawaii on top of it all, and his children aren't even invited?!"

"Wow . . ." I said, feeling a mix of shock, anger, and sadness.

I listened as she continued to talk for several more minutes, venting and becoming surprisingly open and honest with me. After a brief pause, I spoke up.

"Ah, Rachel, I'm so sorry. Honestly, I can't say I know exactly how you feel, because I don't. I haven't had to deal with divorce. And I can only imagine how painful that must be."

She didn't outwardly acknowledge my comment, but she appeared noticeably more comfortable and continued to talk.

"And you know what's worse? When your best friend tells you that you just need to 'smile because it'll help you feel better.'"

I shook my head in disapproval. "Like that helps," I said with empathic sarcasm.

"Seriously!" she continued. "And other people say similar things! 'It could be worse,' or 'you'll get over it eventually.' I'm not stupid. I know I'll get over it eventually. But that's not what I want to hear right now."

"That's so frustrating," I said. "That's the *last* thing you want to hear when you're going through something like this."

"YES," she sighed.

For the next hour, we sat in the dim lighting of my car as Rachel completely opened up to me. On top of the divorce, she had been in a car accident just weeks prior (remarkably escaping unscathed), and her younger sister had just been diagnosed with cancer. Divorce, a major car wreck, and a sister with cancer—all in a month. And I sensed this was the first time she was really opening up about it all to anyone.

As we talked, I did what I could to show her that I recognized how she was feeling. Not just that I was listening to her stories and feeling sorry for her, but that I was connecting with her experience. That I saw her pain, and wasn't going to try to fix it, offer advice, or tell her to move on. In that moment, all I could do was help her see that her hurt, anger, and confusion was okay. It was understandable. She had every right to—and very much needed to—*feel it.*

As our evening came to a close, she paused for a moment. "Thank you," she said. "I'm sorry for throwing all that on you. I guess I just haven't really felt like I could talk to anyone about it. This is the first time in a long time that I've actually felt some relief."

I thanked her for being so open with me and walked her to her apartment. As I got back in my car, I sat for several minutes, thinking back on what had just happened. What started as an awkward, one-sided, thirty-minute date ended up being an amazingly connecting and powerful experience. Not only did this new acquaintance come to feel safe confiding in me, I came to feel a very real sense of love, care, and compassion for her. In an hour. Now I'm obviously not referring to romantic love here, but the feeling of seeing and caring about someone on a deeper level. Later that night, I wrote the following in my journal:

> "It was so amazing to see how she just opened up, how she felt safe, and how she, I believe, felt my love for her because I knew how to *validate* her. I could tell it was like a breath of fresh air. That she could finally breathe. That she felt *heard* and *understood.*"

MY 'AHA' MOMENT

That experience was a turning point for me. I saw more clearly than ever before just how powerful validation could be and I was beyond excited.

I first learned about validation—which is, in essence, the act of helping someone feel heard and understood—from my therapist and life coach. I met with her twice a week, in both one-on-one and group settings, over the course of several years, and worked through everything from work drama to relationship issues to day-to-day stressors. Her approach to counseling and coaching focused on teaching people how to live honest, powerful, and *connected* lives. (Side note: I'm now of the opinion that everyone should have a good therapist. Seriously. Life-changing). I quickly found myself waist deep in principles and practices that ran counter to how the majority of the world lives their lives, and the more I practiced them, the more confident and connected I became. Validating, as you may have guessed, is one of those practices.

By the time I went out with Rachel, I was fairly familiar with validation. I knew how to recognize requests for it and I had some experience offering it. What I didn't know, however, was how *starved* people are for it. Seeing how it almost magically melted away Rachel's walls of anger, frustration, and hurt was eye-opening, to say the least.

Over the months that followed, I had similar experiences with family, friends, and colleagues. Topics of conversation ranged from dating and marriage to major business decisions, and I found myself navigating many of these exchanges with clarity and connection.

As I continued to practice this newfound skill, the benefits became more and more noticeable. People began saying things like, "You're so easy to talk to" and "You're a great listener." After observing several of my interactions with others, one of my mentors said to me, "You really have a gift for putting people at ease." Coworkers told me they appreciated how approachable I was as a manager and how impressed they were with how I handled interpersonal and interdepartmental conflict.

I share these comments not to stroke my ego but to illustrate the fact that 1) the skill of validation has noticeable and far-reaching effects, and 2) it's a skill anyone can learn. What these people saw in me was something I had learned, not something I'd instinctively known how to do. Realizing that I'd stumbled onto something quite valuable, I began searching for ways to share it with others. Knowing how to validate was improving nearly every area of my life—my friendships, my conversations with co-workers and my boss, my dating life, my family relationships, and even my interactions with strangers. I had to pay it forward.

While I found several short articles online that touched on validation, I was unable to find anything that taught it on the level and in the manner I felt was most practical. There are books on everything from how to swear effectively to crafting with cat hair (no joke), yet very little on the versatility and power of validation. So, short of recommending four years of therapy to people, I was having a hard time figuring out how to share the wealth.

About six months after my date with Rachel, I received a call from my brother. He was going through a bit of a tough time and was looking for some advice. He filled me in on the situation and then paused. My first impulse was to jump right in with a solution, but, as I thought back to my recent experiences with validation, I felt like there might be a better approach. I put my advice aside and simply said, "Man, I'm sorry. That's gotta be *super* frustrating. I remember dealing with something similar to that just last month and yeah . . . it's rough."

Sure enough, that simple comment helped my brother release a significant amount of frustration. When he spoke next, the relief was already audible in his voice. He shared with me his thoughts on the situation and how he intended to handle it. To my surprise, he was already considering the very solution I was planning to offer. It seemed that, even though he called asking for advice, all he was really looking for was validation. We talked for a few minutes longer, then wrapped up. He told me he felt significantly better and thanked me for taking the time to chat. As I hung up the phone, I sat for a moment and reflected.

"This whole validation thing is amazing," I thought.

Then came the thought I *never* expected.

"What if I wrote a book about it?"

"*Funny,*" my inner critic shot back, "who are you to write a book?"

Yet the thought persisted. As odd as it may sound, I almost felt *compelled* to write something—like I owed it to somebody. I felt selfish for not sharing with others the principles that were so clearly benefiting my life.

"I'm not an author, a researcher, or a therapist," I thought. "Why would people even listen to what I have to say?"

Honestly? They may not. Yet as the days and weeks went by, it seemed that every experience, every conversation, and every moment of silent reflection pointed back to writing this book. I had to write it. I had to at least *try* to pay it forward. If one other person benefited from the attempt, it would be worth it. Finally, one sunny Saturday morning, I opened my laptop and began to write.

INTRODUCTION

WHAT TO EXPECT FROM THIS BOOK

So, no, I'm not a psychologist. I haven't counseled celebrities or big-shot CEOs, and I do not have professional letters after my name. Honestly, I doubt I'm any different from you in terms of intellect, talent, or ability. What I do have to share, though, is the knowledge and insight I've gathered from over four years of therapy and coaching, and ridiculous amounts of trial and error. I've compiled insights and best practices from over a dozen related books, distilled key principles from over 500 hours of discussion with licensed professionals, and have practiced, tweaked, and proven these approaches thousands of times over. You may have to trust me a bit until you get into it yourself, but I assure you: this is good stuff.

As you've no doubt noticed, this book is pretty short. I was tempted to add additional (read: unnecessary) chapters, stories, and other fluff in an effort to make the book longer, because a longer book looks more impressive on the shelf, right? Yet few things bother me more than reading a book that takes 300 pages to explain something that could have been covered in fifty. This will not be one of those books.

Instead, I'm going to get right to the point so you can get on to actually trying things out. Because, when it comes right down to it, the only way to know that the principles in this book are as powerful as I say they are is to try them. Practice them. Apply them. I've included stories and research where I felt they added value and held back where I felt they would not. My goal has been to make this book a quick read; something you can blaze through in a weekend and revisit as needed.

Now, before we dive in, know that these principles will not suddenly fix every problem in your relationships, cure you of all disease, or make you better looking. But they *will* improve your relationships, increase the likelihood that people listen to your advice, enhance your ability to support others during difficult times, and help you more easily navigate emotionally charged situations. I've seen them work magic in my own life and in the lives of countless others. Time and time again, these principles come through. If you take them seriously, you will not be disappointed.

PART I

THE POWER OF
VALIDATION

CHAPTER 1
WHY THIS IS WORTH YOUR TIME

"Being listened to and heard is one of the greatest desires
of the human heart. And those who learn to listen are
the most loved and respected."

– Richard Carlson

Most people will read the above quote and say, "Sure,
people like to be listened to—no surprise there. If I'm a good
listener, people will love and respect me more." While that may
be true, there's a little more to it. Notice the second (and, I
would argue, more important) part of that first sentence:
"Being listened to *and heard* is one of the greatest desires of the
human heart." That distinction suggests that there's a
difference between being *listened to* and being *heard*, and that we
as humans crave both.

Have you ever talked to someone who clearly heard the
words you were saying, but didn't seem to get what you meant?
Or maybe they understood your point, but were obviously
disconnected from the emotion or weight of the situation?
That person listened to you, but didn't really *hear* you. Now, I

know that hearing is technically a sense (i.e., our ears allow us to hear sound), but colloquially, we often use the phrase, "I hear you" to mean "I understand you" or "I get where you're coming from." It's that kind of hearing—a true understanding and connection—that we crave.

So that begs the question: how do you show someone you really hear them? This is where things get interesting. The truly good listeners of the world do more than just listen. They listen, seek to understand, and then *validate*. That third point is the secret sauce—the magic ingredient.

DON'T JUST LISTEN, *SAY* SOMETHING

I dated a woman a while back who was great at listening but *terrible* at validating. As I would relate an exciting or difficult experience to her, she would often sit there with an unemotional look on her face and, when I finished talking, look at me as if to say, "Anything else?"

I hit a breaking point one evening after sharing something I was particularly excited about. As I finished the story (and calmed down a bit, as I tend to get quite animated in my storytelling), I looked at her and saw that same rather blank look on her face. "Cool!" she said.

And that was it.

I paused for a moment longer, expecting her to follow up with "That's so exciting!" or "Then what did you do?" or *something* that showed me she actually cared about what I had just shared. I had been talking for several minutes, so a one-word response was surely not all she was going to give.

Nothing.

She just looked back at me with that same plain (though pleasant) look on her face and eventually asked, "What?"

Okay. What was going on here? She listened to my story, didn't interrupt, and seemed pleasant enough in her one-word response. What was I expecting?

What I was expecting—and quite literally craving at this point in our relationship—was validation. I wanted to feel like she saw, understood, and shared in my excitement. I wasn't telling her the story because I liked talking; I was sharing it with her in the hope that she would see my excitement and get excited *with* me. I was hoping we would connect over the shared experience.

As I returned home that evening, I did as any healthy, productive, responsible human being would do and started mindlessly scrolling through Facebook. After a few minutes, I came across a link to an article on Business Insider titled "Science Says Lasting Relationships Come Down to 2 Basic Traits." Intrigued, I clicked through and began to read.

The article discussed studies conducted by psychologist John Gottman who, for the previous four decades, had studied thousands of couples in an effort to figure out what makes relationships work. Seeking to better understand why some couples have healthy, lasting relationships while others do not, Gottman and his colleagues decorated their lab at the University of Washington to look like a beautiful bed and breakfast. They invited 130 newlywed couples to spend a day at the retreat and watched as they did what most people do on a typical weekend—prepare meals, chat, clean, and hang out.

As Gottman studied the interactions of each couple, he began to notice a pattern. Throughout the day, partners would make small, seemingly insignificant requests for connection from each other. For example, a husband would look out the window and say, "Wow, check out that car!" He wasn't just commenting on the car, though; he was looking for his wife to respond with shared interest or appreciation. He was hoping to connect—however momentarily—over the car. Gottman calls these requests for connection "bids."

The wife could then choose to respond positively ("Wow, that *is* nice!"), negatively ("Ugh, that's hideous"), or passively ("Mmm, that's nice, dear"). Gottman refers to positive and engaging responses as "turning toward" the bidder, and negative and passive responses as "turning away." As it turned out, the way couples responded to these bids had a profound effect on their marital well-being.

Gottman found that couples who had divorced during the six-year follow-up period had "turn-toward bids" just 33 percent of the time—meaning only three in ten of their requests for connection were met with interest and compassion. [1]

In contrast, couples who remained together after the six-year period had "turn-toward bids" 87 percent of the time. Nearly *nine times out of ten*, the healthy couples were meeting their partner's emotional needs.

Now here's the kicker: by observing these types of interactions, Gottman can apparently predict with *up to 94 percent certainty* whether couples—rich or poor, gay or straight, young or mature—will be broken up, together and unhappy, or together and happy, several years down the road.

As I sat at my computer reading this article, something clicked. A surge of insight and validation (with a hint of vindication) flooded my body. *This* is what my relationship was missing! I was indeed making multiple "bids" or requests for connection each day, but felt like my girlfriend only "turned toward me" a small fraction of the time.

I was familiar with the concept of validation by this time and had become quite adept at offering it to others, but I hadn't yet learned to recognize when *I* needed it. As I read the article, I realized that what Gottman refers to as "turning toward" another individual is simply another way to describe validation—showing interest in and affirming the worth of another person's comments, requests, or emotions.

This new insight opened my eyes to a clear reality: validation is critical for building healthy, satisfying relationships. What's more, it's critical for *any* relationship, romantic or otherwise. Thus, the core idea of this book is that, in order to become a "great listener," you actually need to become a great *validator.*

THE SWISS ARMY KNIFE OF COMMUNICATION SKILLS

A few years ago, I met up with a good friend for lunch. We caught up on recent life events and reminisced about a few of the good times we'd had together. As the conversation progressed, we ended up talking about my recent study and exploration of validation. I had shared some of my research with him a couple of months prior, so both he and I were "trying it out." We shared and analyzed recent experiences, looked for common threads, and sat in amazement at how effective this skill was. Just a week prior, I'd used the Four-Step Method (to be introduced in Part II of this book) to defuse a tense situation at work. In my pre-knowing-how-to-validate days, similar situations would turn into an hour or two of discussion and often end with significant frustration. With my newfound approach, it was resolved in about thirty minutes with all parties feeling heard and understood. As I relayed the experience to my friend, I laughed, shook my head in disbelief, and said, "This feels like a super power!"

Cheesy, I know, but validation was working like a charm. Of course, not every conversation I was having was a life-changing experience, but more often than not, the Four-Step Method delivered. I was learning to help others feel heard and understood, and I was beginning to realize just how desperately people needed that. Add to this the fact that few people even know what validation is, and you can see why this felt like a super power.

With the principles, tools, and techniques set forth in this book, you will be able to:

- **Calm (and sometimes even eliminate) the concerns, fears, or uncertainties of others.** This is especially helpful if your significant other is upset, if you're dealing with irate customers or coworkers, or if you're trying to reason with young children.
- **Add a boost to others' excitement and happiness**. This is an obvious gift to the other person, but studies have also shown that validating the positive experiences of others can drastically improve connection and satisfaction in a relationship.
- **Provide support and encouragement to others, even when you don't know how to fix the problem.** There is great confidence in knowing you can help someone in *any* situation, regardless of your own experience or expertise.
- **More easily show love, understanding, and compassion in your intimate relationships.** Studies (and common sense) show that this skill is critical to lasting, happy relationships.
- **Help others feel safe and comfortable confiding in you.** This promotes deeper, more meaningful connection and increases others' affinity toward you.

- **Avoid or quickly resolve arguments.** Instead of butting heads and going in circles, you'll save time, frustration, and headache by knowing how to calm the other party *and* make your point heard.
- **Give advice that sticks.** When you understand and validate others, they become significantly more open to your advice, feedback, and/or assurance.
- **Become an all-around more likeable human being.** When you help someone feel heard and understood, they can't help but develop a natural liking toward you. Humans have a deep-seated need to feel heard and appreciated. Those who sincerely fill those needs, therefore, are among the most loved and respected.

In other words, this stuff is amazing. And it applies to virtually *any* relationship in your life. If you have coworkers, friends, siblings, parents, children, neighbors, a spouse, a girlfriend, a boyfriend, a hairstylist, a boss, a landlord, or a taxi driver, you can use validation to improve that relationship.

CHAPTER 1 SUMMARY

We want (and need) more than just a listening ear. As humans, we need to feel heard and understood. We need to feel accepted and appreciated. Good listeners, therefore, do more than just listen—they validate.

Validation can make a tremendous difference in your marriage or romantic relationships. Studies show that couples who learn to validate and support each other have significantly happier and longer-lasting marriages than those who do not.

Validation is as versatile as it is valuable. Effective validation can calm fear or frustration, give a boost to others' excitement or good fortune, get others to listen to your side of the story, deepen relationships, quickly resolve arguments, and help make you an all-around more likeable human being.

CHAPTER 2
VALIDATION 101

"Behind the need to communicate is the need to share.
Behind the need to share is the need to be understood."

– Leo Rosten

We as humans are social creatures. We crave acceptance, appreciation, and a sense of belonging. In times of joy and success, we seek to share our excitement with others. In times of pain and sorrow, we seek comfort and support. Whichever way you slice it, we are hardwired for connection. As John Gottman noted in his research, we make dozens—if not hundreds—of requests for connection each day. More often than not (and whether we know it or not), we are looking for validation.

As I mentioned earlier, validation (in the context of interpersonal skills, anyway) is the act of recognizing and affirming the validity or worth of a person's emotions. Essentially, validation means saying to someone, "I hear you. I get what you're feeling, and it's perfectly alright to feel that way."

Effective validation has two components:

1. It identifies a **specific emotion**
2. It offers **justification for feeling that emotion**

For example, let's say you're out to lunch with a coworker. You've finished your meal and are chatting for a few more minutes before heading back to the office. You've noticed that she seems a bit distracted, frequently checking her phone and not being as present and engaged as she typically is. Curious, you ask what's up.

"Oh . . . my daughter was supposed to call me when she got home from dance practice," she says, "but I haven't heard from her. I was expecting to hear from her an hour ago, so I'm a little worried."

What would you say? Would you offer reassurance? (e.g. "Oh I'm sure she's fine. You know how teenagers are. She probably just forgot.") Or would you jump in with advice? (e.g. "You should call one of her friends!") While both these responses might help, they would be even more effective if you first took a moment to validate. (We'll get to why this is the case in just a minute).

To validate your coworker in this situation, you would hold off on the advice and assurance for a moment and instead say something like, "I don't blame you for being worried, especially if she told you she'd call an hour ago..."

Notice how that response 1) identifies a specific emotion (worry), and 2) offers justification for feeling that emotion (it's been over an hour since she expected to hear from her daughter). This response shows your friend that you not only hear how she's feeling, but that you understand *why* she's feeling that way. While it may seem counterintuitive, choosing to validate your friend instead of offering solutions to her problem is likely the best way to help.

A study published in 2011 illustrates this point. Participants were asked to complete a number of difficult math problems during a short period of time, and then asked to report their emotional state (e.g. stressed, embarrassed, confident, etc.). The facilitator then responded with either a validating or invalidating comment. If the participant expressed frustration, for example, the researcher would respond with a comment such as, "Whoa, other people were frustrated, but not as much as you seem to be" (invalidating), or, "I don't blame you— completing math problems without pencil and paper is frustrating!" (validating).

Participants were then asked to complete a second round of arithmetic and once again report their feelings. Their emotions were once again validated or invalidated, and the process was repeated a third and final time. Researchers measured participants' response to the stress and feedback by tracking their heart rate and skin conductance levels (SCL), common measures of physiological response. When the experiment was complete, the data was gathered and analyzed, and trends, correlations, and insights recorded.

Perhaps unsurprisingly, participants who received invalidating responses showed a gradual increase in SCL, a prolonged stress response, and a steady increase in heart rate. They also reported regular increases in negative feelings after each round, despite being told "not to worry." In other words, they *were* worrying, and they really weren't enjoying the experiment.

Participants who had their emotions *validated*, however, had entirely different results. These individuals showed a significantly lower trajectory of SCL, reported nonsignificant changes in negative feelings, and actually showed a steady *decrease* in heart rate over the course of the experiment.[2] Did you catch that? It wasn't just that their heart rate stayed flat, or rose at a slower rate than those who were invalidated; it actually went *down*, despite the fact that they continued to work through difficult problems. While they were exposed to the same stressors as the other group, those who had their feelings validated found it significantly easier to regulate their emotions and keep their cool.

More often than not, people who vent or complain already know how to handle their current situation—they're just looking for someone to see and appreciate their struggle. While it seems almost counterintuitive, validation is often the quickest and easiest way to help people work through their concerns and get back on track.

VALIDATING RESPONSES

There are, of course, countless ways to validate. As long as you show the other person that you recognize and accept their emotions, you're validating. Any of the following comments would be validating in the appropriate context:

- "Wow, that *would* be confusing."
- "He really said that? I'd be angry too!"
- "Ah, that is so sad."
- "I totally get why you feel that way; I've been in a similar situation before and it was *rough*."
- "You have every right to be proud; that was a major accomplishment!"

- "I'm so happy for you! You've worked incredibly hard on this. It must feel amazing."

Notice again how each of these responses refers to a specific emotion and shows some justification for or acceptance of it. Including both elements of validation shows the other person that you not only hear them, you *understand* them.

INVALIDATING RESPONSES

Now that we're familiar with basic validating responses, let's take a look at their more commonly employed sibling: *in*validating responses. Invalidating responses are often born out of good intentions, but they do anything but help.

Society teaches us from an early age that there are certain emotions that we "should" and "shouldn't" feel. Comments such as "don't cry," "don't worry," and "don't be angry," as well as "be happy," "be more confident," and "just enjoy the journey" all reinforce this idea. For some reason, we've grown uncomfortable with certain emotions and labeled them as "bad." These often include worry, fear, anger, jealousy, pride, sadness, guilt, and uncertainty. At the same time, we're told that we need to feel more of the "good" emotions. These typically include happiness, excitement, calm, confidence, and gratitude.

This may seem fine and dandy on the surface, but it starts to become a problem when we feel bad about ourselves for feeling a "bad" emotion. If I shouldn't get angry—but I do—then maybe I'm a bad or angry person. If I'm worried about something that I shouldn't be worried about, then maybe I'm irrational or overdramatic. If I'm afraid of something that I shouldn't be afraid of, then perhaps I'm weak or a coward. These and other shame messages run rampant through our minds, all because we aren't feeling the way we "should."

The truth is *there's nothing inherently good or bad about any emotion*. Emotions just are. They're simply reactions to a situation. And, whether we like it or not, we're going to feel a whole slew of them, each and every day, for the rest of our lives. William Shakespeare's character Hamlet said it best: "There is nothing either good or bad, but thinking makes it so." It is how we interpret these emotions—and choose to handle them—that makes the difference.

Anger, for example, gets a bad rap. While many let it lead them to violence, others let it lead them to positive action. Many of the most significant, positive changes in this world came about because someone became angry about an injustice and let that anger drive them to do something about it.

So how does this judging of emotions relate to validation? Put simply, it completely undermines it. When we tell people they should or shouldn't feel something, we risk making the situation worse. Think back to the study from the last section: telling participants to not worry (or otherwise suggesting that they were being irrational) *added* to their stress. Unfortunately, invalidating others is easy to do. For most people, it's almost a knee-jerk reaction. How many times have you responded to a friend or family member with some variation of the following?

- "You'll be fine."
- "It could be worse!"
- "At least it's not [fill in the blank]."
- "Just put a smile on your face and tough it out."
- "Don't worry; things will work out."

- "Stop complaining; you're not the only one who's hurting."
- "It's not that big of a deal."

If you're anything like me (or most people), one or more of these phrases probably sounds all too familiar.

"But what if there's really nothing to worry about?" you ask.

It doesn't matter. What matters is that the other person *is* worrying and wants someone to see and appreciate that. Everyone—regardless of age, gender, or IQ—will find themselves in a similar situation from time to time, when they're stressed or worried about something they "shouldn't" be. When someone is in that state, a simple "don't worry" doesn't help. If you instead show them that you see and appreciate what they're feeling, they'll either find a solution of their own, or become much more willing to listen to yours.

KNOWING WHEN TO VALIDATE

While everybody likes the feeling of validation, very few people know about it by name. They can sense when they are or aren't receiving it, but rarely do they know what to call it. As a result, it's unlikely that someone will approach you and outright say, "I could use a little validation." So this begs the question: how do you know when to validate?

Requests for validation are far more common than you might expect. In my experience (admittedly lacking any form of scientific measurement), 80-90 percent of conversations have at least one opportunity to validate. In other words, if someone is talking to you, they're probably hoping for validation. This again stems from our basic human need for appreciation and acceptance. It's something we all feel an inner draw towards, regardless of how independent, confident, or self-sufficient we may be.

If you're uncertain about whether you should validate, simply check to see if the other person is sharing something. It could be an experience, an emotion, a concern, etc. If someone is sharing something with you (e.g. "You'll never believe what happened at work!" "I just don't know what to do with Aaron." "This upcoming exam is going to kill me!"), they are probably looking for validation. Even if they share an issue with you and ask for advice, they will still be hoping (consciously or unconsciously) for a little validation first.

The remaining 10-20 percent of your conversations will be factual in nature with little-to-no emotion involved. If the other person is asking for directions, assigning a project to you at work, or asking what you'd like for dinner, you're probably in the clear. But if a person asks for directions, *and then tells you he's worried he's going to get lost*, he is once again looking for validation.

EXAMPLE #1: FRUSTRATED SPOUSE

The following example is adapted from a conversation a friend of mine had with his wife. She came to him frustrated with her sister and looking for support.

Amy: "Ugh. Emily is driving me crazy!"

David: "What happened?"

Amy: "You know this sisters' trip we've been planning? She keeps changing the plans and doesn't seem to listen to—or care at *all* about—what the rest of us want to do."

David: "Well, have you just told her what you want to do?"

Amy: "Of course I have. We all have! She always seems to have some reason for doing things her way. Ugh. I'm so sick of this."

David: "You should just tell her that—that you don't feel like she's listening."

Amy: "I've *tried* that. She always does this. I feel like I'm crazy because everyone else just backs down and lets her take over. I'm not about to spend all this money and take a week off work only to have to follow her strict schedule all day!"

David: "Well, if you don't want to go, don't go."

Amy: "Of course I want to go! I just want to go and actually have *fun*!"

David: "Then just talk to your other sisters. I'm sure you guys can figure it out. Or *I'll* talk to her!"

Amy: "No, I can take care of it. I'm just frustrated."

David: "What if you each planned one day?"

Amy: "It's not that easy. The sites we want to see are too far apart from each other."

David: "What if you just booked a tour group instead?"

Amy: "No, we want to do it ourselves."

David *(not quite sure what Amy is expecting from him at this point)*: "Well, you'd better figure it out soon. Isn't the trip in a few weeks?"

Amy *(now frustrated and ready to end the conversation)*: "Yeah. It's okay. I'll figure it out."

Why did David's multiple attempts to help his wife go so poorly? In short, he didn't recognize that she was looking for validation rather than advice. Amy remained frustrated because David tried to fix the problem right out of the gates instead of first validating her frustration. David also walked away feeling confused and unappreciated because Amy became *more* upset—and even a little defensive—as he tried to help.

Again, David's best chance of helping his wife would have been to simply acknowledge that her frustration was understandable and refrain from offering advice unless she asked for it. What makes the situation extra tricky, though, is the fact that Amy wasn't even aware that she was looking for validation. All she knew was that as her husband tried to reassure her or offer solutions, she became increasingly defensive.

Here's how the conversation might have played out had David validated Amy instead of immediately trying to reassure her:

Amy: "Ugh. Emily is driving me crazy!"

David: "What happened?"

Amy: "You know this sisters' trip we've been planning? She keeps changing the plans and doesn't seem to listen to—or care at *all* about—what the rest of us want to do."

David: "Really? What's up with that?"

Amy: "I don't know! It's driving me crazy. The trip is in a few weeks and I'm afraid we won't be able to get reservations."

David: "Ugh, that's so frustrating. What are you going to do?"

Amy: "I don't know. She always does this. I feel like I'm crazy because everyone else just backs down and lets her take over. I'm not about to spend all this money and take a week off work only to have to follow her strict schedule all day!"

David: "Well, *yeah*—you're splitting everything four ways, right? It's your vacation as much as it is hers."

Amy: "Seriously. I'll figure it out. It's just so frustrating."

David: "Yeah, that really would be. Especially if you keep running into this with her."

Amy: "I do! I've just come to expect it from her. Ever since we were kids."

David: "That would drive me crazy."

Amy: "Ugh, *tell me about it!*"

David: "Ugh, I'm sorry."

Amy: "It's okay. I think I'll just talk to her about it again. If she really won't budge . . . I don't know. I might even do my own thing when we get out there."

David: "Not a bad idea. Hopefully she loosens up a bit."

Amy: "Yeah."

[Brief pause]

Amy: "Anyway, thank you for listening. How was work?"

David's response in this example employs several principles of validation that we'll discuss later in this book. He recognized that Amy was looking for validation rather than advice and offered just that. The result is simple, respectful, nonjudgmental support that helps Amy talk through and let go of her frustration rather than trying to ignore or suppress it. Their conversation becomes much more pleasant and connecting, and leads to a significantly more positive outcome.

EXAMPLE #2: FEELING INSECURE

Let's say you're talking to a friend who has been feeling insecure about her looks. After a particularly hard day, she plops down on your couch and sighs.

"I'm never going to get a guy to date me."

Most people's knee-jerk reaction would be to shoot the comment down, insist it's not true, and proceed to build their friend up with plenty of praise and encouragement. Would you have done the same? Even if that was your initial impulse, you've probably read enough of this book by now to suspect that there's a better approach. (And that suspicion would be correct).

Say you do shoot back with something like, "That's not true! You're totally going to find someone." That wouldn't be a bad response. Heck, you might be afraid that if you *don't* say something like that, she'll think you *do* think she's a lost cause. But let's be real here for a second: if you immediately respond with, "that's not true," will it really make her feel any better? Will she have a stroke of insight and say, "oh, okay, thank you!" and then go on her merry way?

Not likely.

A response like that might take the edge off for a second or two, but it's not going to have any sort of lasting effect. Even if you, her coworkers, her family, and every person she ever talks to insist that she is beautiful, fun, smart, etc., it doesn't change the fact that she *feels* unattractive in some way. There are countless accounts of professional models (we're talking people who literally get paid because everyone thinks they're gorgeous) admitting to feeling ugly and unlovable. In cases like these, there's something deeper going on, a reason why the person is feeling the way they are. And if we're being real here, the only way for your friend to truly feel lovable is to work through those issues and feelings.

Here's where validation becomes so valuable. As we discussed earlier, it's very difficult for someone to work through difficult issues when they're blinded by strong emotions. Painful or difficult emotions get stronger and more intimidating when fought or suppressed. When you validate other people, you help them see and accept their emotions for what they are: just feelings—neither good nor bad. This makes it significantly easier for them to process them and break free.

So how do you validate in a situation like this? If you aren't going to just shoot your friend's comment down and try to build her up, then what do you do?

Get curious about the situation. Ask questions to understand the emotion she is feeling and where it's coming from. She could be feeling hurt, embarrassed, sad, angry, or any other mixture of emotions. We'll walk through a few tips and techniques for uncovering someone's feelings later in the book, but a more validating response might look like the following:

Friend: "I'm never going to get a guy to date me."

You: "What? Why do you say that?"

Friend: "I just see all these beautiful women everywhere and I'm nowhere near as pretty."

You: "There are a lot of beautiful women here. It's hard to not compare yourself to others."

Friend: "Yeah. It sucks."

You: "Why do you feel like you're not as beautiful?"

Friend: "Jay said something the other night that really got to me…"

You can see from this example how validation, paired with a little curiosity, can start to uncover the root causes of someone's feelings. In this instance, curiosity and empathy led to some insight about why your friend is feeling insecure. This additional insight will enable you to offer deeper validation in the areas that will have the most impact, and put you in a better position for offering feedback, advice, and assurance.

EXAMPLE #3: STRUGGLING TO HAVE CHILDREN

During the first few years of my parents' marriage, starting a family was among their greatest desires. They wanted nothing more than to be parents and to raise a loving, happy family. Yet, as weeks, months, and soon years passed without a successful pregnancy, it became apparent that having children of their own was going to be much more difficult than they expected. Despite repeated visits to doctors and trying numerous fertility treatments, they were unable to conceive, and the fear that they might never have children of their own grew darker and more frightening. Mother's Day was particularly difficult for my mom, as it served as an annual reminder that she didn't—and may never—have what she wanted most: to be a mother.

As my parents sought support from friends and family, many replied with some form of the following:

- "I'm sure it'll happen eventually!"
- "I wouldn't worry about it too much. It'll all work out if it's supposed to."
- (And my personal favorite): "You can't have kids? My husband just *looks* at me and I get pregnant!"

The people who made these comments may not have intended to be hurtful or dismissive, but their responses demonstrated a lack of empathy and minimized the pain and fear my parents were facing. It didn't take long before my parents stopped confiding in these individuals and turned instead to those who were better at empathizing and validating.

In this situation, a more validating response would have been any of the following:

- "I'm *so* sorry. I can't even imagine how hard that must be."
- "You know what? I haven't been in your exact situation, but I can relate. Rick and I struggled to have kids for over five years and I still remember the agony I felt. There's nothing easy about what you're going through."
- "Ah, that's *so* hard. I'm sorry. How are you feeling?"

VALIDATING VS. INVALIDATING RESPONSES

Before we wrap this chapter up, let's round out our understanding by taking a quick look at some side-by-side comparisons of validating vs. invalidating responses. Each example consists of one comment and two possible responses—one validating and one invalidating. These are short, sweet, and to the point, but if you're looking for a little extra credit, take a moment or two to think up a few additional validating responses for each situation.

Comment: "I'm worried about this upcoming exam . . ."

Invalidating Response	Validating Response
"Don't be! You'll do great. I'm sure of it."	"I don't blame you! This is a hard class!"

Comment: "This cold is *so* annoying! I can't sleep, I have a hard time breathing, and my throat is killing me."

Invalidating Response	Validating Response
"That's unfortunate, but you'll get over it. It could be worse—my neighbor caught the flu last year and was bedridden for almost a month!"	"Ugh, that sounds miserable. It's so frustrating not being able to sleep when you're sick, and I can't *stand* sore throats."

Comment: "I don't want to go to school anymore. I'm so embarrassed after last night's talent show that I don't ever want to show my face there again!"

Invalidating Response	Validating Response
"You have nothing to be embarrassed about. You did a great job!"	"I'm sorry, honey. It's tough getting up there in front of the whole school like that—especially when you're performing. Is there anything specific you're worried about?"

Pretty straightforward, right?

Congratulations! You've just completed Validation 101. You now have a solid understanding of the basics and are ready for a more thorough—and actionable—deep dive. Chapters 3 and 4 will clear up common misconceptions (citing interesting research and personal experience) and give you a crash-course on empathy to set you up nicely for the powerful principles in Part II.

CHAPTER 2 SUMMARY

Validation has two main elements. It 1) acknowledges a specific emotion, and 2) offers justification for feeling that emotion.

Validation is nonjudgmental. It allows the other person to feel whatever they're feeling without labeling it as "good" or "bad."

*In*validation (i.e. minimizing or dismissing another person's feelings) is counter-productive. Research has shown that invalidating responses can make a difficult situation worse, even when offered with the best of intentions.

Offering validation—before or instead of offering advice or assurance—is often the best way to help. Doing so helps others let go of difficult emotions much more quickly, often allowing them to find a solution to the problem on their own. Leading with validation also increases the likelihood that others will listen to and accept your advice.

CHAPTER 3
COMMON MISCONCEPTIONS

"Connection is the energy that is created between people
when they feel seen, heard, and valued."

– Brené Brown

While the basic concept of validation is quite simple, I often
see it underutilized or misapplied due to a few common
misunderstandings. May as well clear those up right now.

MISCONCEPTION #1: VALIDATION IS ONLY FOR NEGATIVE EMOTIONS

We've talked a lot about negative emotions up to this point,
but validation is just as beneficial in supporting positive
emotions. In fact, research has shown that the ability to
validate the positive experiences of others can drastically
improve connection and satisfaction in a relationship.

In a study conducted in 2004, researchers found that
romantic relationships were higher in commitment,
satisfaction, trust, and intimacy—and lower in daily conflict—

when partners validated each other's good fortune.[3] No real surprise there, though, right? That's what you'd expect.

What researchers were surprised to find, however, was that passive–constructive responses (e.g., "That's nice. Guess what happened to me today!") had the same correlation with negative relationship outcomes as active *destructive* responses (e.g., "You got promoted? Say goodbye to sleep!"). In other words, responding to someone's excitement with an obvious lack of interest, even if your comment is positive, may be just as harmful as responding with a negative, discouraging comment.

Suppose a woman and her husband are relaxing in their backyard after a long day. The woman, catching up on email, suddenly turns to her husband and says, "I just got the nicest email from my boss!" Her husband, without even looking up from his smartphone, says (in a pleasant, but obviously disconnected tone), "that's nice, honey," and continues reading. The wife, knowing her husband isn't really paying attention, turns back to her computer and continues flipping through messages. How appreciated do you think she felt by her husband in that moment? You've likely had a similar experience, and it's not hard to see how failing to validate positive emotions can be hard on a relationship.

Now, consider how the situation could have played out had the husband recognized his wife's request for connection and validated her excitement:

"I just got the nicest email from my boss!" says the woman.

"Really?" the husband replies, looking up from his phone.

"Yeah, listen to this: 'Jane, I just wanted to let you know that I continue to be impressed with how well you manage the wide variety of projects you're in charge of. You are a key player on the team and I don't know how we could have landed those accounts last week without you. Keep up the great work.'"

"That's fantastic!" the husband responds.

"Seriously," his wife replies, beaming. "I don't think I've ever received a compliment from him before."

"That's got to feel nice. You must be doing something right!"

The couple chit-chats for a few seconds longer, then they each return to their respective devices. It amounts to a simple exchange, but the little things add up.

Opportunities to validate positive experience are all around. If we're not attentive, however, they're easy to miss. Most people recognize opportunities to help a distressed friend or family member, but it often feels less important to focus the same amount of attention on another's excitement or good fortune.

I had a powerful reminder of this just the other day. I stopped by a fast-food restaurant on my way home from work, and as I waited for my dinner, I noticed a little boy and his dad sitting at a table across the way. The boy was working on a 3D puzzle that came with his kids' meal and his dad was sitting across from him, staring into his smartphone. That scene alone was sad (I mentally pleaded with the dad to put his phone away), but when the little boy finished his puzzle, the situation became even more unfortunate.

As the boy clicked the last piece into place, his eyes lit up. A huge grin spread across his face and, with great pride and excitement, he held it up for his dad to see. My heart sunk as I watched the dad respond with an unenthusiastic, "that's cool!" without even looking up from his smartphone. My eyes darted back to the little boy. He looked at his dad for half a second longer, obviously hoping for some sort of acknowledgement or positive validation, then looked back down at his toy and continued playing.

That was hard for me to watch—not only because that young father missed an opportunity to validate and connect with his son, but because I know I have been guilty of similar behavior. The little boy didn't complain or even say anything, but his "bid" or request for connection was left unmet. Had the father put his phone down, taken a closer look at his boy's puzzle, and said something like, "Wow, nice work! Those puzzles are hard!" he would have sent a very different message. And it would have taken only a few moments of his time.

Validating positive experience is not only possible, it's critical to developing healthy, satisfying relationships. Learning to identify and act on these opportunities can make a significant difference in your connection with others.

MISCONCEPTION #2: YOU CAN'T VALIDATE IF YOU DON'T AGREE

When you validate someone, you're essentially saying, "I get why you're feeling the way you are." It's important to note that this is *not* the same as saying "you're right" or "I agree." You can validate any emotion in any situation as long as you understand the other person's perspective. While it may not seem like it at first, most people's reactions (even the seemingly irrational ones) make perfect sense once you truly understand where that person is coming from. You may need to think about their background, their fears, their hopes, the fact that they might not have all the details, etc., but more often than not, you'll find that their response is actually quite reasonable given the situation.

Years ago, a coworker came into my office and asked to talk. He sat down and began to express concern that another coworker, whom I had put in charge of a few rather menial tasks, was underqualified and might produce work inconsistent with our brand.

I listened as this coworker expressed his concerns. After a moment or two, I tried to jump in and assure him that I had it taken care of. My reassurance appeared to go in one ear and out the other, though, and he then expressed concern about *my own* creative experience and ability.

A feeling of wounded pride began to well up inside me as I fought to keep my cool and avoid getting defensive. Despite my efforts, it wasn't long before I began listing for him my education and experience in a futile attempt to convince him that I did, in fact, know what I was doing.

After a couple attempts to make him feel better in this way (while also defending my ego), I realized it wasn't working. He continued to restate his original points over and over and continued to raise new concerns. We were talking in circles, and he clearly wasn't hearing me.

Then, I took a step back and realized I was handling this all wrong. I had jumped right to trying to fix the problem before acknowledging and validating his concerns. He wasn't hearing *me* because I wasn't hearing *him*. I paused for a moment, listened closer to what he was saying, and tried to understand what he was feeling. I realized that, from the limited information he had, he *did* have reason to be concerned.

I paused for a moment, and then said, "You know what, Jace? I can absolutely see why you're concerned. Without hearing all the discussion and project details, you just see this guy suddenly working on projects for which he's *not* the most qualified. I whole-heartedly agree with you there. You're basically left to wonder who's driving these projects, if you'll get to have any say in the creative direction, etc. I'd be concerned too if I were in your shoes."

"*Yeah*," he said, the relief audible in his voice. "That's exactly it. I'm just concerned that he doesn't have the experience and skill for these types of projects."

"Aha!" I thought to myself, "progress!" Recognizing that one validating comment had finally broken us out of the endless cycle of argument, I continued:

"I totally get why you're concerned, and I very much appreciate your keeping an eye out for the company. I also appreciate you bringing this up to me, as I know these kinds of conversation aren't easy to have."

"Yeah seriously, Michael," he said with an even deeper sigh of relief. "I don't think you have any idea how hard this is for me to have this conversation with you right now."

By this point, the tension in the conversation had eased significantly, and Jace, now feeling heard and understood, was finally open to my perspective. I explained to him that I too felt this individual was not the best fit for the position, but that he was qualified *enough* for these particular projects. I assured Jace that I would be working closely with this person to ensure quality work and that I wanted Jace's help in executing a few key elements.

"Thank you, Michael," he said, "that is what I needed to hear. I feel much better about this now." He left my office and we carried on with our work.

Notice how (after a little trial and error on my part), I was able to validate Jace's concerns without ever saying, "You're right. He shouldn't be working on this." If I hadn't paused to understand and validate his concerns, our conversation could have continued for hours with little or no resolution.

If someone is distraught, angry, or concerned, validating them is your best chance at getting them to be receptive to feedback. The great thing is, you can validate someone even if you disagree with them. Learning to do so will give you a valuable tool for navigating confrontations, negotiations, disagreements, and the like.

MISCONCEPTION #3: VALIDATION IS SIMPLY REPEATING WHAT THE OTHER PERSON SAYS

Years ago, I learned of a technique called reflective listening. Reflective listening is essentially the act of repeating back to someone, in your own words, what they have just said. The idea here is that you 1) check to see if you've heard them correctly, and 2) help them realize you are listening. While this can be a useful skill, I've found that it is frequently misunderstood and poorly implemented. If you're not tactful, simply reflecting back what someone has said can come across as mechanical and inauthentic.

If a friend tells you she's angry because her boss insulted her, a reflective listening response might be, "You feel angry because he insulted you." It's factual (as far as you know), nonjudgmental, and shows your friend that you're paying attention. Reflective listening focuses on the words the other person has just said.

Validation, in contrast, focuses on the *emotion* the other person has just expressed. As we discussed in chapter 1, most people don't question whether we understand their words; they want to know that we're *connecting* with what they're sharing. For the example above, a more validating response might be, "Wow! I'm angry just hearing about that!" The key difference here is that rather than looking *at* your friend's experience, you're getting into it *with* her and seeking to understand how she's feeling.

Several years ago, I enrolled in an interpersonal and communication skills class where students were encouraged to keep in touch with each other outside the classroom. A couple of classes focused on empathy and validation, and we were encouraged to follow up with each other as we practiced these principles in our day-to-day lives.

One class member, however, mistook validation as reflective listening, and when he tried to offer validation, it felt mechanical and impersonal. When I would call him up, looking for a little support or a fresh perspective, our conversations sounded something like the following:

Me: "Hey Tyler, I'm feeling really frustrated right now. Do you have a second?"

Tyler: "Yeah, what's up?"

Me: "I just spent eight hours on a project at work only to find out that the criteria changed and I have to start over. I'm feeling a ton of stress and frustration right now and just need some help letting it go."

Tyler: "Hmm, so let me see if I got this right. You're feeling frustrated right now. You spent eight hours on a project for work and then found out that you have to start over? I also heard that you're feeling stressed and wanted to call someone who would help you let it go. Is that right?"

(I'm not exaggerating here. That's really how he talked.)

Now, there's not necessarily anything *wrong* with that approach (at least I knew he was listening!), but it didn't feel sincere. To be honest, it was a little awkward. I sat there thinking, "It's like I'm talking to a script-reading tech support agent right now!"

With the best of intentions, this guy was simply repeating back what I had told him without connecting to how I was feeling. It didn't help that he repeated back my words nearly verbatim—something even reflective listening experts advise against. It's not surprising that I felt the lack of empathy and our conversation fell flat. The more validating response I was hoping for would have gone something like:

"Wow, you spent *eight hours* on that? What happened?" [...conversation...] "Gosh, I'm sorry, that's super-frustrating."

Effective validation requires empathy and emotional understanding, and therefore extends beyond simple reflective listening. We need to do more than just show others we hear the words they are speaking; we need to show them we're connecting with the emotions they're feeling.

CHAPTER 3 SUMMARY

You can validate any emotion—positive or negative. While validating difficult emotions can lead to stronger, healthier, more satisfactory relationships, studies have shown that validating positive emotions and sharing in others' excitement, pride, happiness, etc. can be equally beneficial.

You can validate anyone, even if you disagree with them. When you validate someone, you're essentially saying, "I get why you feel that way." That's different than saying, "You're right" or "I agree." The key point here is that if you were in that person's shoes, having only the information, background, and perception that they do, you would likely feel the same way.

Validation is more than just repeating what the other person says. Simply reflecting another's words, without seeking to understand the emotion behind them, can come across as inauthentic and disconnected. While rephrasing what you've heard is a valuable tool, validation shows an understanding of the other person's emotions and the "why" behind them.

CHAPTER 4
IT ALL STARTS WITH EMPATHY

"Could a greater miracle take place than for us to look
through each other's eyes for an instant?"

– Henry David Thoreau

Before diving into the Four-Step Validation Method, it's
important to ensure we have a basic understanding of
empathy—the foundation of genuine connection. Empathy is
the ability to understand and share the feelings of another.
When we have empathy for another person, we put ourselves
in their shoes and feel what they are feeling. We seek to
understand where they are coming from and try to imagine
what they are going through.

EMPATHY IS DIFFERENT FROM SYMPATHY

Sympathy is a feeling of care or concern for another person,
often accompanied by a wish to see them better off or happier.
Sympathy is standing on the *outside* of a situation, looking in

(e.g. "I'm sorry you're sad.") Empathy is stepping *into* the situation and feeling the emotion (e.g. "Wow, this *is* sad.").

When we sympathize, we feel *for* someone because of his or her pain. When we empathize, we feel the pain *with* them. For example:

Sympathy	Empathy
"I'm sorry you're not feeling well."	"Ugh, the flu is no fun at all."

Sympathy	Empathy
"I'm sorry you're frustrated. I hope you figure it out."	"Ah, that's so frustrating!"

In a talk given at a conference in 2013, author and research professor Brené Brown gave an example that helps further illustrate the difference between sympathy and empathy.

Imagine, for a moment, that someone has fallen into a dark hole. They look up and say, "I'm stuck. It's dark. I'm overwhelmed."

Brown suggests that a sympathetic response would be to look down into the hole and say, "Whoa! That's bad. I'm sorry you're down there. Do you want a sandwich?"

In contrast, the empathic response would be to climb down into the hole *with* them and say, "I know what it's like down here. It's tough. And you're not alone."[4]

Effective validation can come only after we've connected with the other person and are able to understand—at least to some extent—what they are feeling.

TIPS FOR DEVELOPING EMPATHY

Struggling to feel empathy for someone? While there's no sure-fire, one-size-fits-all approach to developing it, the following tips may help.

Empathy Tip #1: Get Curious

Ask yourself the following questions:

- "What is this person's background? Could past issues be influencing their reaction?"
- "What if someone had done that to me? How would I feel?"
- "If I haven't had a similar experience, have I ever felt a similar emotion?"
- "What if that were *my* [child/parent/job/dog/etc.]?"

Asking questions such as these often uncovers an element or two of the other person's circumstance that strikes a chord inside you.

Empathy Tip #2: *Look* at Them

Pause for a moment, let go of whatever thoughts may be zipping through your head, and take a moment to truly *see* the person across from you on a deeper level. Make eye contact. Recognize that they are a human being with fears, hopes, uncertainties, pain, and joy. Recognize that their life may be a lot harder than you know.

This can be a surprisingly powerful experience when done with sincerity. Taking time to recognize that another person may be hurting, or may be especially excited or hopeful about something, will help you get out of your own head.

Empathy Tip #3: Imagine Them as a Child

This may sound odd, but imagining another person as a young, vulnerable child often makes it easier to feel their emotion. If you're having a hard time empathizing with your roommate during an embarrassing situation (perhaps you think he should "just get over it"), consider how you would feel if you looked over and saw a four-year-old standing there with fear, shame, and embarrassment visible on his face. I have been guilty of telling a genuinely scared friend to "man up" even though I would never have said such a thing to a terrified four-year-old.

Imagining others as younger, more vulnerable versions of themselves is a great way to help feelings of empathy flow a little more freely.

Empathy Tip #4: Learn to Identify Your Own Emotions

You can't feel empathy for another person if you don't know how they're feeling. Yet being able to accurately identify others' emotions isn't always as easy as it may seem. The good news is that you can improve your ability to recognize others' emotions by making a habit of identifying your own. Again, this may sound simple, but you might be surprised.

For example, how are you feeling right now?

If you're like most people, you'll probably say, "fine."

But "fine" isn't an emotion. It's how you're *categorizing* your current emotion.

"Okay," you say, "I'm feeling *good*."

Nope. Still not an emotion.

"Right. I'm feeling *happy*."

There we go. Happy is an emotion, and something others can relate to. If you tell me you're feeling "good," I'll probably assume you mean "content," and I may or may not be right. If you tell me you're feeling "happy," I now have a much better idea of where you're at and can more accurately relate.

One way to practice identifying your own emotions is to set a reminder on your phone to check in with yourself a few times throughout the day. Then take these moments to pause, notice how you're feeling, and identify the emotions by name. Keep an eye out for the following cop-out responses:

- "Good"
- "Fine"
- "Better than yesterday"
- "Alright"
- "Okay"
- "Not great"

When you catch yourself using a cop-out word or phrase, dig deeper for the actual emotion. For example:

- "Good" might actually mean: happy, grateful, comfortable, content, excited, energized, confident, or positive.
- "Okay" might actually mean: content, tired, worn out, or worried.

- "Not great" might actually mean: scared, hurting, sad, lonely, worried, betrayed, sick, uneasy, anxious, or weak.
- "Better than yesterday" could really mean anything: happy, comfortable, excited; or sad, anxious, etc.

Learning to identify your own emotions will increase your ability to feel empathy for others in two ways. First, you'll become hyper-sensitive to cop-outs when you hear them from others. I find myself keying in on these responses all the time now. I'll be at work, the grocery store, or out with friends, and ask someone how they're doing. Nine times out of ten they'll say "good," and I'll feel an almost knee-jerk reaction to dig a little deeper. "Just good?" I'll often ask. Their response to my follow-up is almost always more genuine and detailed, which sets the stage for a more authentic (and more enjoyable) conversation.

Second, getting in the habit of identifying your own emotions helps you build a broader catalog of emotional experience. When someone tells you they're feeling embarrassed, you'll be better able to empathize if you can think back to a specific moment when you felt the same way. If you haven't been in the habit of identifying your own emotions, those same embarrassing experiences will likely end up filed away in the "bad feelings" folder in your mind and be much more difficult to access.

Empathy Tip #5: Quit Judging Your Own Emotions

In order to have empathy for others, you need to identify *and accept* their emotions without judgment. It's not easy to do this for others if you're not already in the habit of doing it for yourself. Unfortunately, as discussed in chapter 2, many of us grow up believing that certain emotions should be suppressed, avoided, or ignored. If you see this tendency in yourself, I have good news: you're already well on your way to changing it. The more awareness you can bring to the habit, the easier it will be to change it.

The next time you notice an emotion—any emotion—rising up inside you, check to see if you're suppressing, avoiding, or accepting it. How will you know if you're avoiding it? Simply look for invalidating statements. Are you telling yourself to "suck it up" or "stop worrying"? Are you trying to convince yourself that "it's fine"? These are telltale signs that you've judged the emotion instead of accepting it. Once you've noticed that you are avoiding or repressing, you have an opportunity to stop, step back, and practice accepting instead.

When you notice an emotion come up, try to look at it as objectively as possible, like a scientist observing a reaction:

"Man, I'm ticked."
"Huh, I'm feeling a lot of jealousy right now."
"Wow, I'm actually feeling pretty sad."

For extra credit, you can even practice validating yourself:

"Okay, I'm upset. That makes sense. He promised he would be on time and he's already fifteen minutes late. Who wouldn't be upset?"

The more you practice recognizing, accepting, and validating your own emotions, the easier it will be to develop empathy for, and then validate, the emotions of others.

CHAPTER 4 SUMMARY

Empathy is different from sympathy. Sympathy is standing on the *outside* of a situation and looking in (e.g. "I'm sorry you're sad.") Empathy is stepping *into* the situation with the other person and feeling the emotion *with* them (e.g. "Wow, this *is* sad").

Empathy Tip #1: Get curious. Ask yourself questions such as, "What is this person's background? Could past issues be influencing their reaction? What if someone had done that to me? How would I feel? If I haven't had a similar experience, have I ever felt a similar emotion?"

Empathy Tip #2: *Look* at them. Take a moment to see the other person on a deeper level. Make eye contact. Recognize that they are a human being with fears, hopes, uncertainties, pain, and joy. Recognize that their life may be a lot harder than you know.

Empathy Tip #3: Imagine them as a child. Try picturing the other person as a four-year-old version of themselves. Because showing emotion is considered a sign of weakness in many cultures, it can be difficult to empathize with adults who may be having a hard time. Picturing the other person as a young child can help remove this stigma and make it easier to feel genuine empathy.

Empathy Tip #4: Learn to identify your own emotions. Become better at identifying others' emotions by getting in the habit of identifying your own. Consider setting a reminder in your phone each day to check in with yourself and take inventory of how you're feeling.

Empathy Tip #5: Quit judging your own emotions. The next time you notice an emotion—any emotion—rising up inside you, check to see if you're suppressing, avoiding, or accepting it. The more you practice recognizing, accepting, and validating your own emotions, the easier it will be to develop empathy for, and then validate, the emotions of others.

PART II

THE FOUR-STEP
VALIDATION METHOD

INTRODUCTION TO PART II

While the concept of validation is relatively simple, knowing how to effectively implement it in your day-to-day can be a bit more difficult. The Four-Step Validation Method is a tried-and-true approach to giving validation and feedback in nearly any situation. I reverse-engineered it from thousands of successful validation experiences and boiled it down to four basic steps. Each step is accompanied by several key principles that provide additional insight and direction.

The Four-Step Method is simple by design, allowing it to apply to everything from quick, lighthearted exchanges to lengthy, emotionally charged conversations. Because every interaction is unique, the way you implement the method will vary from case to case. In nearly every situation, however, the Four-Step Method will help you better connect with and support the other person. We will explore several examples of implementing the method in Part III.

Like riding a bike or playing an instrument, the skill of validation will become second nature with practice. You will not always need to think, "Step 1 . . . Step 2 . . . Step 3 . . ." every time you talk with someone. With practice, you will comfortably and naturally flow through and adapt the method without giving it a second thought. Let's get into it.

THE FOUR-STEP
VALIDATION METHOD

1. Listen Empathically

2. Validate the Emotion

3. Offer Advice or Encouragement (if appropriate)

4. Validate the Emotion Again

STEP 1
LISTEN EMPATHICALLY

"One of the most sincere forms of respect is
actually listening to what another has to say."

– Bryant H. McGill

Before you can validate someone, you have to first understand how they are feeling. This starts with listening, but also requires you to look beyond the words they speak and identify the emotions they express. This is known as empathic listening.

Author and mediation expert Gregorio Billikopf notes that empathic listening "requires that we *accompany a person* in her moment of sadness, anguish, self-discovery, challenge (or even great joy!)."[5] [Italics added]

As you listen to others, employ the empathy-building techniques discussed in the previous chapter. Ask yourself, "What emotions do I see in them? Are they angry? Hurt? Excited? Confused? How would I feel?"

Get curious about the situation. Show your interest by asking clarifying questions and checking to see if your observations are accurate, such as:

- "That was last week, right?"
- "So then what did you do?"
- "Wait, she actually said that to you?"
- "How did that feel?"
- "You seem worried."
- "You sound frustrated."

The better you understand the situation and how the other person is reacting to it, the more effective your validation will be.

KEY PRINCIPLES: EMPATHIC LISTENING

Give Your Full Attention

In today's fast-paced, ever-connected world, we have dozens of distractions vying for our attention. You might think that as long as you *seem* attentive in a conversation, it's okay to let your mind work on other things. Nothing could be further from the truth. When we're not fully present, people notice.

Have you ever had the experience of talking with someone whose mind was obviously elsewhere? Maybe they kept glancing at their phone, looking over your shoulder, or checking the time. It's tough to feel like you matter to them in that moment. Whatever they're distracted by, it's apparently more important than talking to you. Not a great feeling.

Olivia Fox Cabane, author of *The Charisma Myth*, points out that "not only can the lack of presence be visible, it can also be perceived as inauthentic—which has even worse emotional consequences. When you're perceived as disingenuous, it's virtually impossible to generate trust, rapport, or loyalty."[6]

If someone asks to talk when you're distracted or unable to take a break, let them know and ask if you can talk at a later time. You might say:

"I'm sorry, I'm right in the middle of a stressful project and would be distracted if we talked right now. Can I call you in an hour? I want to give you my full attention."

When you do talk with them, show them they have your undivided attention. Close your laptop, even if your screen is blank. Take your ear buds out, even if music isn't playing. Turn the TV off, even if it's muted. These little actions go a long way in boosting your presence. Not only do they help you avoid distraction, they show the other person that you care about them enough to focus entirely on them.

If you're questioning whether or not these actions really make that much of a difference, consider this: research has shown that the mere *presence* of a smartphone can lessen the quality of a conversation—even if it's just sitting on the table. No joke. In a 2014 study dubbed "The iPhone Effect," researchers paired up 200 participants and invited them to sit down in a coffee shop and chat with each other for about ten minutes. Research assistants observed the conversations from a distance and paid special attention to whether a mobile device was used, touched, or placed on the table during the conversation. When the time was up, participants were asked to respond to a series of questions and statements designed to measure feelings of connection, empathic concern, and the like. These included, "To what extent did your conversation partner make an effort to understand your thoughts and feelings?" and "I felt I could really trust my conversation partner."

The results?

If either participant pulled their phone out or placed it on the table, the quality of the conversation was rated to be less fulfilling compared to conversations that took place in the absence of mobile devices.[7] "Even when they are not in active use or buzzing, beeping, ringing, or flashing, [digital devices] are representative of people's wider social network," the researchers note. "In their presence, people have the constant urge to seek out information, check for communication, and direct their thoughts to other people and worlds."

True, undivided attention is rare in today's world. If you value the person you're speaking with more than the latest sports score or a new text message, *show them*. Trust me—it will make a difference.

Invite Them to Open Up

It's not always easy to walk up to someone and say, "I'm frustrated right now. Can I talk it over with you?" Instead, many people "hint" that they want to talk, using comments such as, "I'm so frustrated right now," or "Ugh, it's been a really tough week."

In other cases, the person's body language and overall energy will signal that something is up. If you're in a good place and wanting to help, you can show them you're willing to listen with a simple invitation:

- "You seem upset. What's up?"
- "Do you want to talk about it?"
- "What's going on?"

If the person wants validation and support, a simple, casual invitation like this is often all they need to begin talking. If, after a little encouragement, they still don't want to talk, don't pry. You've let them know that you are willing to listen, which is a gift in and of itself.

Be Observant

When it comes to communication, we can't (and don't) rely solely on the words others say. Communication experts suggest that as much as 70 percent of our communication is nonverbal—meaning it's delivered via body language, tone of voice, etc. [8]

Chances are you've had at least one experience with saying one thing when you actually felt another. That little voice inside our heads often tells us to bend the truth to avoid burdening or offending others. As a result, you say, "Nah, I'm fine," when you're not. You agree to help a friend, saying "Sure, I'll do that," and then sulk in the knowledge that you're going to be late for work. You tell your spouse it's "no big deal" that they ate your leftover cake, when deep down you're ready to strangle them.

Because of this tendency, it's helpful to pay attention to people's expressions, tone of voice, and body language as they speak. Does what you see and feel fit with what they're telling you? Do your observations give you additional insight into what else they may be feeling?

I once had dinner with a woman who shared bits and pieces of a pretty rough childhood. She never once said "it sucked" or "it was really hard." She just relayed a few of the facts as she tried to keep a smile on her face.

She didn't have to say, "I felt abandoned" or "It was incredibly painful." I could see it in her eyes. I tried to empathize with her, imagining the difficulty of what she had just shared with me.

"Wow," I said, feeling a mixture of sadness and respect, "that must have been *really* tough."

"Yeah," she admitted, pausing for a moment, "it was."

The conversation soon moved on to happier topics, but by taking a moment to look past her words and connect with her emotion, our friendship grew ever-so-slightly stronger.

Match Their Energy

Imagine for a moment that you just won a cruise for two from an online sweepstakes. (Now imagine that it's legit—not one of those telephone scams.) Excited out of your mind, you approach a friend at work.

"You'll never believe this!" you exclaim, "I just won an all-expense-paid trip to the Caribbean!"

"Really?" your friend responds, lacking the energy and excitement you were expecting.

"Yeah! I can't believe I actually won! I never win anything!"

With a half-smile and a look that makes it obvious that he doesn't really care, your friend says, "Wow, that's awesome. Congrats."

That's a bit of a letdown, right? It doesn't really matter what your friend said to you; if he said it in a less-than-enthusiastic way, you'd feel deflated. Even if he was genuinely happy for you, the fact that he didn't match your energy (in this case, your excitement) would lead you to believe that he doesn't really care.

This is consistent with the findings of the study discussed in chapter 3, where researchers discovered that passively supportive reactions (i.e., quiet, understated support) were just as harmful to a relationship as actively destructive reactions (i.e., deliberately shooting down the other person's thoughts or feelings).

Matching another person's energy is a critical part of effective validation. If the person is excited, then smile, laugh, and share in the thrill. If the person is sad, then be respectful and speak in a softer, more compassionate manner. This principle comes naturally to many people but can be easy to forget when you're distracted, stressed, or otherwise preoccupied. By matching the other person's energy, you'll be viewed as more present and connected to what they're saying and feeling.

Offer Micro Validation

Micro validation is a short comment or response that affirms the validity of the other person's emotions, opinions, etc. These quick, simple comments let the other person know that you are following what they're saying, that you're not judging them, and that they're safe to continue sharing. Like matching energy, most people do this automatically.

Micro validation looks like the following:

- "Really??"
- "Uh, yeah, I'd be angry too!"
- "Wow, that must be so frustrating."
- "That makes sense."
- "That's so exciting!"
- "No way."
- "I can see that."
- "Wow, that must have hurt."
- "I can see how that would be confusing."
- "Congratulations! That must feel amazing!"

The goal here is to keep the comments short so they don't feel like an attempt to interrupt or take over the conversation.

As insignificant as these comments may seem, they play a major role in keeping a conversation moving. Imagine talking to someone who didn't react at all to what you were saying. It wouldn't be much different than talking to a brick wall, and you certainly wouldn't be talking for long.

Micro validation lets the other person know you're paying attention and encourages them to continue sharing. It also fosters a sense of safety and trust. They're opening up to you on some level (whether they're relating a positive or negative experience), and micro validation helps them feel safe in doing so.

Don't Try to Fix It

If someone is venting or sharing a negative experience, do not jump in with advice unless they ask for it. Similarly, resist the urge to point out silver linings or how the situation could be worse. **This is—by far—the most common mistake people make.** As we discussed early on, statements such as the following—no matter how well intentioned—*invalidate* the other person's experience:

- "That's not true—you look great!"
- "Here's what you need to do . . ."
- "Don't worry about what they think."
- "Hey, just let it go! It's not worth letting it ruin your day."
- "It will all work out in the end."
- "It could be worse."
- "Don't worry. You'll meet the right person some day."

Giving unsolicited advice or assurance—especially before you validate the other person's emotions—trivializes their experience. It suggests that 1) you don't think they should feel the way they do, and 2) you know how to resolve the issue better than they do. Even if you *do* know how to resolve it, now is not the time to say so. While it may be true that it's not worth getting all bent out of shape over what's happened, the fact is that the other person *is* bent out of shape over it and they need someone to understand why.

This is far easier said than done, but learning to hold off on giving advice will make a tremendous difference in the amount of trust and safety you build in your relationships. This is not to say there's no place for feedback or advice in a conversation; this is simply not the best time. You will have an opportunity to offer advice, feedback, and/or assurance in step 3, and waiting until then will increase your chances of being heard.

STEP 1 SUMMARY

Give your full attention. If you're distracted, let the other person know and ask to talk at a later time. When you are available to talk, close your laptop, turn off the TV, and keep your attention on the conversation at hand.

Invite them to open up. If you suspect someone wants to talk about something but isn't comfortable initiating the conversation, try asking a simple question like, "You seem upset. What's up?"

Be observant. As much as 70 percent of our communication is nonverbal. Pay close attention to the other person's tone of voice and body language to better understand them.

Match their energy. If the other person is happy or excited, then smile, laugh, and share in the thrill. If they are discouraged or sad, then be respectful and speak in a softer, more compassionate manner.

Offer micro validation. Offer short comments such as "no way!", "seriously?", or "I'd feel that way too" to help the other person feel comfortable sharing. This lets them know you that you are listening, withholding judgment, and seeing things from their perspective.

Don't try to fix it. Refrain from offering advice, feedback, or assurance until step 3. Avoid comments such as "at least . . . ", "you should . . . ", or "that's not true."

STEP 2
VALIDATE THE EMOTION

"The most important thing in communication
is hearing what isn't said."

– Peter Drucker

Once there's a pause in conversation or the other person is done sharing, move onto step 2 by offering more direct validation. You will remember from chapter 2 that validating responses acknowledge or give worth to the other person's comments or emotions by:

1. Identifying a **specific emotion**
2. Offering **justification for feeling that emotion**

If you say, "I get that you're worried," you're offering simple validation by showing the other person that you are listening and understand. If you then show the other person that you understand *why* they are feeling worried, the effect of that validation multiplies. For example: "I get that you're worried. It would be tough not to be given the situation."

Consider the following additional examples:

- "Seriously, I'm so happy for you! You put a *ton* of work into that presentation. It must feel amazing that it went so well!"
- "You have every right to be frustrated. I'd go *crazy* if I spent four hours on something only to find out that I was headed the wrong direction the whole time."
- "I get why you're confused. Last week I told you one thing, and today I'm telling you something that seems to be entirely different."
- "I get why that would hurt. There you are, at the happiest moment of your life, and your friend didn't show up to support you. It probably felt like he didn't even care."

KEY PRINCIPLES: VALIDATING THEIR EMOTION

Still Don't Try to Fix It

Yes, this is a repeat principle from step 1. It still applies. I'm including it again because jumping straight to advice or assurance remains the number one temptation for, well, just about everyone.

You Don't Have to Agree to Validate

We've talked about this before, but remember that you do not need to agree with the other person to validate them. If you feel like they aren't seeing things correctly, don't pretend to agree—but also don't tell them you *disagree* just yet. Instead, try to understand why they're feeling what they're feeling and validate that. Try to see things from their perspective. If you only had their side of the story, chances are good that you would react in a similar way.

For example, say that a coworker complains to you about being passed up for a promotion.

"I don't get it," he says, "I deserve that promotion far more than Drew! I've been here nearly twice as long!"

If you're anything like me, your first reaction will be to immediately challenge that comment. Does he really think he deserves a promotion simply because he's been working for the company longer? Oh, the entitlement! But let's pause for a second and put ourselves in his shoes.

How would you feel in this situation? Frustrated? Confused? Angry? Embarrassed? Maybe all of the above? It would be confusing and disheartening to think that you were next in line, and then see a newer team member get promoted before you. So even though *you* may not think this guy deserves that promotion, you can at least understand why he would feel like he does. In this step, it's important to hold back your judgment and opinion and focus solely on validating. Doing so in this situation will 1) reduce the likelihood that you get into an argument, and 2) improve your coworker's willingness to listen when you *do* share your perspective in step 3.

You could validate your coworker, without suggesting that he deserves the promotion, by saying something like, "I get why you're upset. You've been here longer than anyone! It'd be tough to see someone else get that promotion."

Not Sure What They're Feeling? Ask.

If you're having a difficult time figuring out what the other person is feeling (perhaps they're in the habit of hiding or downplaying their emotions), just ask. This takes a bit of finesse so as to not sound like a psychiatrist (e.g., "how do you *feel* about that?"), but the following two techniques can help you identify someone's emotions without sounding like you're trying to psychoanalyze them.

Option 1: The "Keep it Casual" Approach

In this approach, ask the person what they're feeling directly, but in a casual, non-intimidating way. This requires only minor tweaks to avoid sounding like a therapist:

- "So, how are you feeling about all this?"
- "Ugh. How'd *that* make you feel?"

Simple yet effective.

Option 2: The "Guessing/Asking" Approach

In this less direct approach, throw out a few emotions you think they may be feeling in question form:

- "So, are you feeling frustrated? Confused? Angry?"
- "So, you must be excited? Nervous? A mix of both?"

This technique has two benefits. First, it shows the other person that you're listening and trying to connect with them. Second, it helps them identify their emotions, which ultimately gives you something to validate. The Guessing/Asking approach tends to play out in a way that's similar to one of the following:

You: "So, are you feeling frustrated? Confused? Angry?"

Friend: "Yeah, I'm frustrated because it feels like no matter what I say, they don't take me seriously."

You: "I don't blame you. That would drive me crazy."

If your guesses about what the person is feeling aren't accurate, they will likely correct you and provide clarification:

You: "So, are you feeling frustrated? Confused? Angry?"

Friend: "No, I actually don't care about it at all to be honest. I guess I just feel betrayed since she promised me she wouldn't do that."

You: "That makes a lot of sense. I'd feel the same way."

If You Can Relate, Let Them Know

If you can relate to what the other person is sharing with you, step 2 is a good time to consider letting them know. Done tactfully, this can strengthen your validation and foster greater trust and connection.

A word of caution: If someone is sharing a difficult emotion or experience, avoid the phrase, "I know *exactly* how you feel," even if you think you do. Instead, consider phrases such as, "I've felt *similar* when . . ." or "I can relate to that feeling."

Claiming to know "exactly" how someone feels nearly always puts the other person on defense. If you don't believe me, pay attention to your reaction the next time someone says it to you. Even with the best of intentions, it is a surprisingly *in*validating thing to hear.

In truth, none of us know exactly how another person is feeling. Our thoughts and emotions are shaped by millions of life experiences, to the point where it's virtually impossible for any two people to have the *exact* same thoughts or reactions. If you can relate, simply avoid using "exactly" and you'll be in a good spot. It's a small change, but when emotions are running high, the devil is in the details.

Several years ago, a friend came to me racked with emotion after a painful breakup. The hurt and frustration he expressed sounded oh-so-familiar as I reflected back on a recent breakup of my own. Realizing I could relate to much of what he was saying, I continued listening until he was done sharing, then responded with the following:

> "I'm sorry. That's really tough. I can actually relate. That sounds a lot like how I felt when Sarah and I broke up. Every time I ran into her I felt a pit in my stomach and wanted more than anything to get back together. The next several weekends *sucked*. It's tough feeling like you're back at square one again, right?"

Sharing my own experience was validating because the emotions I had experienced were very similar to what my friend was feeling. But notice how I quickly relayed my experience and then turned the focus back to my friend by asking him a question. This is important when sharing your own experience. Had I just ended it with "the next several weekends sucked," the focus would have been left on me, making it harder for him to continue sharing.

When you use a personal experience to validate, keep it brief, focus on the emotions and experiences that are most relatable, and then return the focus to the other person.

If You *Can't* Relate, Let Them Know

While having had a similar experience can certainly help you relate to and feel empathy for another person, it's not necessary. Believe it or not, acknowledging the fact that you *can't* relate can be one of the most validating things you can say. Why? Because it shows respect and appreciation for the other person and their situation. It's the opposite of "I know exactly how you feel" and it's surprisingly validating.

To validate in this way, acknowledge the emotions the other person has expressed and think about what you might feel in the same situation.

For example, while you may never have had to deal with the death of one of your own children, you can almost surely imagine, at least to some extent, the intensely heavy feelings of despair, longing, regret, anger, and fear that would accompany such a loss. You can offer validation and show respect with comments such as:

- "I honestly don't know what to say. I can only imagine how painful that must be."

- "Oh my gosh. I am so sorry. I can't even imagine what you must be going through right now."

This is how I approached the situation I shared in the introduction. The woman I was out with was going through a difficult time with her parents' divorce—something I did not have personal experience with. Instead of pretending to know what she was going through, I acknowledged the fact that I didn't. When she saw that I responded with validation rather than advice, she quickly lowered her walls and we were able to connect on a much deeper level.

The power of this kind of validation is incredible. Not only does it validate the other person's emotions, it also demonstrates respect by not trivializing their experience. Admitting that we don't know exactly how another person feels helps them feel safe in confiding in us. They come to realize that they can be vulnerable with us without facing judgment or pressure to fix the problem.

Tell the Truth

From time to time, friends and family will come to us feeling embarrassed, regretful, frustrated, etc. because they've made a mistake, underperformed, or are simply in a tough spot. In these situations, it can be tempting to sugarcoat the truth to avoid adding to their pain. This often results in our telling the other person, "You did great!" when they didn't; "I think it turned out well," when we don't; or "He doesn't know what he's talking about," when we know he does.

The problem with beating around the bush or sugarcoating the truth is that the other person likely *knows* the truth and can tell when we're not being honest. Again, they've come to us because they're looking for validation, not for help burying their uncomfortable emotions.

When you're faced with such a situation, acknowledge the truth and the difficulty of the situation. You can be tactful about it, but you don't have to lie. Consider the following example of Trent, a seventeen-year-old high school student who faced a difficult situation during his state championship soccer game.

Trent is an excellent player, often scoring multiple points in a game. In this particular game, however, he let a few opposing players get inside his head. On his first goal attempt of the game, Trent slipped right before taking the shot and completely missed the ball. The opposing team heckled, jeered, and taunted him, which got to him after a while. Trent took shot after shot at the goal but missed every time. He turned the ball over to the opposing team far more often than usual. His coach took him out for a time to help him regain his composure, but as he sat on the bench, the negativity and frustration over his poor performance weighed heavier and heavier on his mind. His team lost the game and Trent walked away feeling like it was entirely his fault.

As he approached his dad at the sideline, he looked at the ground and shook his head. "I just lost the freakin' championship for my team."

How would you respond? If you're like most people, you'd immediately fire back with a compassionate, "No you didn't! You did a great job!"

There are two problems here, though. First, this is an invalidating statement. Did you catch it? Immediately responding with "no you didn't" discounts the feelings Trent just expressed rather than allowing him space to feel them.

Second, Trent *didn't* do a great job—and he knows it. As a result, he'll likely dismiss altogether any suggestion to the contrary, no matter how well-meaning. Is he solely responsible for losing that game? No. Did he play hard? Absolutely. But did he play well? Not particularly, *and that's okay*. He's human. We all have off days. If we try to dismiss or change his emotions, however, we reinforce the idea that it's *not* okay to make mistakes and feel frustrated.

A more validating response would be as follows:

Dad: "I'm sorry, Trent. That was definitely a rough game."

Trent: "I can't believe I couldn't make *one shot!*"

Dad: "You weren't on your A-game tonight, and sometimes there's nothing you can do about that. I'd be just as frustrated. *And* I hope you realize that the loss isn't entirely your fault."

Trent: "I know, but I just can't believe I lost my cool like that."

Dad: "What do you mean?"

Trent: "I let the other players get in my head!"

Dad: "What happened?"

Trent: "It was all because of that stupid first shot. The other team wouldn't shut up about it for the whole game, and I couldn't stop thinking about it! I felt humiliated."

Dad: "I'm sorry, Trent. That would be embarrassing. And frustrating to not be able to move past it."

Notice how Trent's dad acknowledged the fact that Trent didn't play well while also showing empathy. His response will likely align well with what Trent is saying to himself (i.e., "I didn't play well and this sucks"), which helps him feel heard and validated. His dad was also able to gain some additional insight into *why* Trent didn't play his best, and validate the fact that messing up like that in front of his peers would be a tough thing to shake.

Maintaining honesty and sincerity in your validation not only improves its effectiveness, it also increases trust in the relationship. If your friend always told you you did a great job, even when it was obvious that you didn't, you would learn to disregard his compliments. "He always says that," you'd say to yourself, even when he really did think you did well.

In contrast, if that same friend wasn't afraid to tell you when he wasn't impressed, a compliment from him would hold much more weight. You'd feel confident that he was being genuine, which would make the kudos that much sweeter.

Being honest, yet tactful, in your validation is easier said than done, but it's a worthy pursuit and pays dividends down the line.

STEP 2 SUMMARY

Validate their emotion. Once there's a pause in the conversation or the other person is done sharing, validate them more fully. This is best done by 1) acknowledging the emotions they've expressed, and 2) offering justification for feeling those emotions.

Validate, even if you disagree. Not only is it possible to validate someone you disagree with, it's advantageous to do so. When you validate the other person, they become significantly more likely to listen to a differing opinion or advice. Once you show that you truly *hear* them, they will be much more likely to hear *you*.

Not sure what the other person is feeling? Ask. A simple question such as "How are you feeling about all this?" or "I imagine you're pretty upset?" is often enough to get the clarity you need to validate.

If you can relate, consider letting them know. Use phrases such as "I can relate" or "I had a similar experience" instead of "I know exactly how you feel." Be sure to turn the focus back to them after sharing your experience.

If you *can't* relate, let them know. Acknowledging that you haven't been in someone else's shoes and don't know exactly how they feel can be incredibly validating.

Tell the truth. Resist the urge to lie to make someone feel better. Instead, acknowledge the truth, validate their emotions, then provide comfort and assurance in step 3.

STEP 3
OFFER ADVICE OR ENCOURAGEMENT
(IF APPROPRIATE)

"Whenever you have truth it must be given with love,
or the message and the messenger will be rejected."

– Mahatma Gandhi

Once you have listened to and validated the other person, you are in a good position to offer advice, feedback, or encouragement, if appropriate.

What do I mean by appropriate? Not every situation will warrant feedback. In fact, most of your day-to-day validation opportunities will not. When you do have an opportunity to give advice, it's important to first determine whether or not the other person is open to hearing it.

Avoid Offering Unsolicited Advice

It's easy to assume that since someone is venting to you, they're looking for advice. As we've discussed in earlier chapters, however, this is often not the case. Because of this, launching into unsolicited advice may cause the other person to close off, get irritated, or become defensive. Think back to a time when someone started telling you what to do when all you really needed was someone to hear you out. Been there? Most have. To prevent yourself from committing the same offense, use one of the following two methods to see if the other person is open to feedback.

Approach #1: Ask What They Want from You

If someone has shared a difficult emotion or experience with you but has not asked for help, say something like:

- "How can I help?"
- "Is there anything I can do?"

More often than not, they'll ask for your thoughts. You may find, however, that your listening and validation was all they really needed. They may say, "Well, just having you listen has been helpful" or "You know what? I think I have it figured out. Thanks for letting me vent." It's amazing how quickly people can work through their issues when they feel heard and validated.

Approach #2: Ask Permission to Share Your Thoughts

If you would like to offer feedback and don't want to leave it up to the other person to request it, try some variation of the following:

- "I have a few thoughts on that. May I share them?"
- "Would you like my opinion?"
- "May I tell you how I see it?"
- "Could I share my two cents?"

When you ask permission before sharing your opinion, you show respect for the other person, their emotions, and the fact that they are smart and capable in their own right. If they do give you permission to offer feedback, they are far more likely to listen with an open mind—even if it ends up being difficult to hear. If they don't give you permission, respect that and save for the advice for another time.

There Are Exceptions to the Rule

While asking permission to give advice is recommended in nearly every situation, there will be times when giving unsolicited feedback is appropriate, if not necessary. The following two situations are common exceptions, but are by no means the only ones. Keep the "ask permission" principle in mind, but evaluate each situation as it arises.

Exception #1: When Teaching Children

Parents have a responsibility to protect, support, and teach their children whether those children want feedback or not. While it is still valuable to listen to and validate children before giving counsel, it is not necessary to obtain permission from your four-year-old before you suggest she not touch the hot stove. Similarly, if your teenager is getting into trouble, you have a responsibility to warn them about their behavior whether they ask for your advice or not.

This doesn't mean you *can't* ask for a child's permission. Even for young children, asking permission to share your thoughts gives them an opportunity to request help of their own free will, which often makes them more receptive. If they say no, you can always choose to offer it anyway.

When it comes to giving advice to adult children (i.e., eighteen-plus years old, married, and/or living on their own), it is best to ask. Doing so demonstrates respect and trust and can go a long way in establishing a healthy relationship.

Exception #2: When the Complaint or Anger is Directed Toward You

A second exception to this principle is when the other person is angry with or making accusations about *you*. In these situations, you may need to clarify the situation, your intentions, or your position, whether or not they ask you to.

Even in these tense situations, *you can still validate the other person* by using steps 1 and 2 (Listen Empathically and Validate the Emotion). Helping them feel heard, even if you disagree with what they're saying, can go a long way in easing the tension in the conversation. It also increases the likelihood that they'll listen to your side of the story. It never hurts to ask permission to share your viewpoint (e.g., "I see things differently. May I explain?"), but if the answer is no, you may decide to share it anyway. Because these situations can be especially difficult, let's take a look at an example.

Say you're at work and a colleague from another department approaches you, clearly upset. Your team had been asked to help create some materials for a meeting with one of his clients and had been working hard to reach a near-impossible deadline. The night before, the VP (your colleague's boss) reached out to you directly to let you know that, due to a change in the client's schedule, your team now had an extra week to prepare. Your coworker never got the memo, however, and was still expecting the presentation.

Coworker: "I told you I needed that presentation *yesterday* and my inbox is still empty! I thought I made it clear that this meeting is crucial to maintaining our business! How am I supposed to do my job if you can't deliver on deadline?"

Whoa. You and your team pushed aside every other project to get this presentation done and would have delivered had his boss not given you an extension. Unless you have an inhuman ability to remain calm under any circumstance, your blood is probably already at a boil and you can't wait to set your coworker straight.

While lashing back out and putting your coworker in his place may feel wonderful in the moment, it's not going to do any favors for your relationship. If you implement steps 1 through 3 instead (even though that's probably the *last* thing you want to do), you will have a better chance at resolving the situation in a positive way.

Now, the main issue in this example is a simple lack of communication between your coworker and his boss, so the sooner you can clear that up the better. Step 1 (Listening Empathically) in this situation won't mean just sitting there while your coworker goes on and on about how incompetent he thinks you are. Instead, it can mean asking a simple question:

You: "Did you know that your boss called me last night and told us to hold off?"

Asking a question instead of shooting back with an accusation or personal jab is a great way to help your coworker realize that he doesn't have all the information while still keeping your cool. It also provides a check on your own assumptions to make sure you haven't jumped to any conclusions.

Coworker: "What? No—what did he say?"

You: "He told me the client had a last-minute change of plans and won't be able to make it until next week. He said you wouldn't need the report until next Thursday."

At this point, your coworker is likely feeling more than a little embarrassed. You can use step 2 (Validate the Emotion) to validate his initial frustration, and then go straight into step 3 (Giving Feedback) to clearly express your own anger or frustration. To be clear, I am not suggesting that you justify his outburst or take his accusations lying down. His reaction, while understandable given his ignorance, was still disrespectful. You have every right to stand up for yourself and your team and do not need his permission to do so. Here's how that might look:

Coworker: "Oh . . . I'm sorry, I didn't know."

You: "I get why you would be upset if you felt like we had completely ignored a deadline. *And,* I really don't appreciate you jumping to conclusions and storming in here when my team and I have been busting our butts for you. Next time, please make sure you have all of the information before accusing me or others on the team of being incompetent."

Notice here how you can listen to, validate, and inform your coworker in only a few sentences. The response goes straight from validation to feedback and bypasses the request for permission. In situations where the other person's complaint or anger is directed toward you, it can be appropriate—even necessary—to quickly and clearly share your side of the story.

KEY PRINCIPLES: GIVING FEEDBACK

Once you are in a position to give feedback, advice, or assurance, use the following principles to do so effectively.

Lead with a Validating Statement

When sharing your perspective or giving advice, lead with one more validating statement before jumping in:

- "I totally get why you would feel that way. Here's how I see it."
- "I'm angry just listening to you tell me about it! Have you considered talking to him?"

If the person becomes defensive, return to steps 1 and 2 and validate the emotion. If they've given you permission to share your thoughts but you can tell they're not really open to hearing them, simply leave it at step 2 and let them know you're always willing to listen. (Assuming, of course, you are. If not, you can simply wish them well.)

Watch Out for "Buts"

This simple principle will not only improve the delivery of your feedback, it will significantly improve the quality of your day-to-day conversations. When used to connect two phrases in a sentence, "but" effectively dismisses the first phrase altogether. When giving validation, it can instantly undo all your hard work.

For example, imagine you get a haircut and a friend of yours walks up to you and says:

"I really like what you've done to your hair, *but* . . ."

What is she going to say next? You don't know for sure, but it will probably be something negative. She "likes it *but* . . ." At this point, you've likely forgotten the compliment and are fixated on what will come next.

Now imagine she says:

"I really like what you've done with your hair, *and* . . ."

Now what? What's coming next? You still don't know, but you do know that she likes your new 'do. She could say just about anything she wants, and it wouldn't detract from the fact that she "really likes what you've done with your hair."

She could even say, ". . . *and* I liked it better the way you had it before." That's probably not what you wanted to hear, but it's still far easier to take. You're likely to think to yourself, "Even though she liked my hair better the other way, I'm glad she likes it this way too." (Not that your happiness depends on what other people think of you, but that's a topic for another book.)

When we say, "I get that you're frustrated *but* I don't think he meant to hurt you," we diminish the impact of the first half of the sentence—the validating part—and all the other person hears is "he didn't mean to hurt you."

Make an effort to replace "but" with "and" and you'll be amazed at how it frees you up to speak candidly while maintaining trust and safety in the conversation.

Lead with "I" Instead of "You"

A common mistake people make when giving difficult feedback is launching in with direct "you" statements such as:

- "You're wrong."
- "This is your fault."
- "You don't work as hard as the others."

This isn't necessarily an issue when giving praise (e.g., "you're right," "you did a great job," etc.) but when giving less-than-pleasant feedback, it can feel aggressive and abrasive.

Notice how, by leading with "I" (or a form of "I"), the same feedback becomes much easier to hold:

- "I disagree."
- "I feel like this may actually be your fault."
- "It feels like you don't work as hard as the others."

Leading with "I" emphasizes the fact that you're sharing your perspective and prevents the feedback from feeling like an accusation. This simple adjustment softens the blow of negative feedback, reducing the likelihood that the recipient will become defensive. If you were to say to your coworker, "You were insensitive yesterday," you're probably going to get into an argument. What is or isn't considered "insensitive," after all, could be up for debate.

If you instead say, "I felt like you were insensitive yesterday" or, even better, "I felt *embarrassed* when you pointed out my mistakes to everyone yesterday," it keeps the focus on you. You are sharing how your coworker's comment affected you, rather than accusing him of being a mean person.

"I" statements can be as soft or direct as you need them to be. They work well when giving feedback to everyone from a significant other to a direct report at work. Examples include:

- "I feel like you aren't listening."
- "I feel unappreciated when you say that."
- "I don't think that is a wise move."
- "I've noticed that you do this often."

Avoid Absolutes

Absolutes are terms such as "always," "never," "constantly," etc. If your feedback includes an observation of a habit or tendency, it can be tempting to say "you *always* do this" or "you *never* do that!"

Aside from the fact that each of these statements leads with "you" instead of "I," they are abrasive because they are absolute. While it may be true that the other person has a hard time listening to others, it's highly unlikely that they *never* do. Surely they listen when the doctor reads them their lab results or when their friend is suggesting movies to see. Claiming that someone "always" does something is equally false.

This type of feedback can be softened by leading with "I" as discussed above. Saying "I feel like you always do this" is no longer accusatory. You're simply sharing your perception, which may or may not be accurate.

If you choose not to make this an "I" statement, replace the absolute term with a non-absolute. The phrase "you *always* do this" can become "you do this *often*." The statement "you never clean up after yourself" can become "you *rarely* clean up after yourself." Notice again how these simple changes immediately soften the harsh edges of the feedback.

If you remove the absolute term *and* make your comment an "I" statement, the feedback becomes even easier to accept: "I've noticed that you do this often" (more direct—your observation) or "I feel like you do this often" (less direct—your feeling).

Acknowledge When You Slip

From time to time, you will jump to giving advice without asking permission to do so. It happens. Now that you are aware of the importance of asking permission, chances are good that you'll catch yourself in the act. When you do, it can be beneficial, even validating, to acknowledge it. For example, you might finish your sentence and then say, "*And* I just realized that you didn't ask for my opinion. My apologies." People are so used to getting unsolicited feedback that even this simple gesture of respect can be quite disarming. Chances are also good the person will end up asking for your opinion anyway, allowing you to continue sharing with their permission.

STEP 3 SUMMARY

Offering feedback or advice is entirely optional. Perhaps someone has shared an exciting or proud moment, or perhaps you simply have no advice to give. Validation is healing in and of itself. It is not always necessary or appropriate to give advice.

Avoid giving unsolicited feedback. Just because someone is sharing a difficult experience doesn't mean they are looking for advice. Determine whether they are open to receiving feedback by either 1) asking what they are expecting from you (e.g., "How can I help?"), or 2) asking permission to give advice (e.g., "I have a few thoughts on the matter. May I share?").

If you do give feedback, lead with a validating statement. Even though you just offered validation in step 2, prefacing your feedback with one more validating statement will reiterate the fact that you've heard them and are connected with their experience.

Use "and" instead of "but." Doing so will help you avoid inadvertently negating your validation, comments, etc.

Lead with "I" instead of "You." Using "I" underscores the fact that you are sharing your perspective or opinion. It also lessens the likelihood that the recipient will become defensive.

Avoid Absolutes. When giving difficult feedback, replace absolute terms such as "always" and "never" with softer (and often more accurate) alternatives such as "often" or "rarely." If you do choose to use an absolute term, lead with "I think," "I feel," etc. instead of "you."

STEP 4
VALIDATE AGAIN

"Be generous with encouragement. It is verbal sunshine; it warms hearts, costs nothing, and enriches lives."

– Nicky Gumbel

I realize that dedicating an entire step to "validating again" may seem like a stretch, but this repetition (and the order in which it happens) is important. Whether the other person has shared a positive or a negative experience, it's good practice to wrap the conversation up with one final validating comment. Doing so reminds the other person that, despite everything that may have been said, you still hear and understand them.

Again, if you think back to Gottman's research, this is likely the one thing the other person was hoping to receive in the first place. Taking a moment to re-validate can go a long way in cementing the positive experience. This step is particularly valuable if you gave feedback or hard-to-hear advice in step 3.

Re-Validate the Emotion

By the time you've reached this step, you will have listened, validated, and given feedback or assurance if appropriate. At this point, any conversation around how to fix the problem (or excitement around good fortune) has played out and the conversation will begin to wind down to a natural end. Closing the conversation with step 4 often involves a simple repeat of earlier validation. This might look like any of the following:

- "Ugh, I don't envy you. That really is a tough situation. It sounds to me like you have a good plan, though. Good luck with it!"
- "Well, for what it's worth, I'm impressed with how you're handling things. That really is confusing."
- "Again, my deepest condolences. You're going through a really hard time. Please know that I'm here for you."
- "Wow, high school is rough! I have full confidence that you'll work through this."
- "Hey, congratulations again! I'm really happy for you."
- "Well, I just have to say again, you really killed it out there. You have every right to be proud!"

These simple comments end the conversation on an uplifting and respectful note, even in difficult situations. They are a good way of rounding out the entire validating experience.

Validate Vulnerability

While step 4 generally involves the simple reiteration of your earlier validation, certain situations may benefit from validating the other person's vulnerability as well.

When someone shares a personal experience or emotion with you, they make themselves emotionally vulnerable. They open up in a way that is often uncomfortable in the hope that you will be respectful and understanding. This vulnerability is crucial for developing strong, healthy relationships because it allows us to see past the façades and connect with people on a more authentic and personal level.

When people share a personal struggle, express a deeply held fear, or even just admit uncertainty in some area of their lives, they show a less-than-perfect side of themselves in an effort to find support. In the workplace, people make themselves vulnerable when they raise a concern with their boss, ask to be considered for a promotion, or confront a coworker. In all these situations, people risk a whole slew of negative reactions. That is never easy.

If someone has opened up to you, step 4 is a great time to show your gratitude and appreciation. The following comments are all examples of validating vulnerability:

- "It's not easy to talk about such heavy things. I admire your courage in bringing it up and appreciate that you shared it with me."
- "I really appreciate you opening up to me. It means a lot."
- "It must have been hard for you to come to me about this, so thank you. I sincerely appreciate your openness. Know that I think the world of you."

- "Thank you for saying something. I'm sure it was tough to bring this up, especially since you couldn't know how I would react."

By validating the fact that the other person has opened up to you—and how uncomfortable doing so can be—you show them they can confide in you without fear of judgment or dismissal. This benefits both you and the other person by increasing trust and safety in the relationship.

It *is* worth noting here that validating vulnerability is generally only applicable in more, well, *vulnerable* conversations. Saying "I really appreciate you opening up to me" after your friend tells you she just booked a two-week vacation is going to raise some eyebrows. If you're connected with the situation, you'll know when validating vulnerability is and isn't applicable.

STEP 4 SUMMARY

Re-validate the emotion. Whether you've given advice in step 3 or not, work in one final bit of validation at the end of the conversation. Doing so reiterates the fact that you hear and understand the other person and ends the conversation on a positive, emotionally uplifting note.

Validate the vulnerability. Sharing personal thoughts, experiences, or emotions can be difficult, uncomfortable, and even scary. If someone opens up to you, thank them for it and validate the fact that doing so can be quite difficult.

PART III

PUTTING IT ALL TOGETHER

REAL-WORLD SITUATIONS

"The road to learning by precept is long,
but by example, short and effective."

– Seneca

The Four-Step Validation Method and its accompanying principles may seem like a lot to remember. The reality is, though, that in practice, you can go through them all in less than a minute. It's also important to note that these steps are not a perfect science, nor must they all be followed in every conversation.

In certain situations, steps 1 and 2 (Listening Empathically and Validating the Emotion) may be enough. At other times, you may go through the whole set multiple times. Every situation will be different. You'll know what feels natural and genuine in the moment and, with practice, you'll find that validation becomes second nature.

In this final section, we'll explore a variety of real-world situations (abbreviated here as RWSs for short) to see effective validation in action. Much of my understanding of validation has come through listening to and learning from the experiences of others. While nothing can replace your own personal experience, studying a wide variety of examples can go a long way.

A NOTE BEFORE WE DIVE IN

As we've discussed previously, empathy and sincerity are critical elements of effective validation. Sincerity is conveyed not so much by what we say, but by how we say it. If we make validating statements without empathy and sincerity, the connection will fall flat.

Unfortunately, conveying empathy and sincerity in a book is difficult, if not impossible. As such, you'll need to use a little imagination as you read the dialogue in the following examples. The language and expressions used here may not be what you would say, but try not to get too hung up on the verbiage. Instead, keep an eye out for the principles we've discussed and notice how they are being used—and how you might use them yourself. When it comes to your own application of the Four-Step Method, you'll naturally default to the words and phrases that feel the most genuine and natural to you.

To help you identify the four steps and key principles as they're being used, each RWS will include the notations on the following page.

FOUR-STEP METHOD NOTATIONS
FOR REAL-WORLD SITUATIONS

L = Listening

MV = Micro Validation

V = Validation

AP = Asking Permission to Give Feedback

GF = Giving Feedback

VA = Validating Again

VV = Validating Vulnerability

Trevor is complaining to Jacob about another coworker. In this case, Jacob knows the full story and doesn't agree with how Trevor is perceiving the situation.

> **Trevor:** "Man, I can't *stand* Steven. He just sucks up to Lisa [his manager] and does whatever it takes to get to the top. I've been here *twice* as long as he has. *I* should have gotten that promotion, not him."

> **Jacob:** "Ah, I'm sorry, Trevor. That would be really frustrating." **(L, V)**

> **Trevor:** "I don't get it. I've been here far longer than he has, and I have way more experience!"

> **Jacob:** "Yeah, that's tough. Have you asked Lisa why they decided to promote him instead of you?" **(MV, L)**

> **Trevor:** "No, but I'm sure she'll just say something like, 'He was more qualified for the position' or some other vague answer like that."

> **Jacob:** "Really? You don't think she'll give you honest feedback?" **(L)**

> **Trevor:** "I doubt it. I don't think she likes me much anyway."

> **Jacob:** "Really? That's frustrating. Do you want my opinion?" **(MV, AP)**

> **Trevor:** "Sure."

Jacob: "First off, I have to say, I would certainly be frustrated, confused, and probably pretty demoralized to have worked here as long as you have and be passed up for a promotion. That's tough. I *also* have to say, I have been very impressed with Steven's work. He's made a significant impact since starting here, opened over 200 accounts, and is a pleasure to work with." **(V, GF)**

Trevor: "I work *just* as hard as he does, if not harder!"

Jacob: "You certainly work hard—no question about that. It's hard to know why he got it instead of you without asking Lisa." **(MV)**

Trevor: "I'll ask her in my next meeting."

Jacob: "Sounds good. Hey, I'm headed into a meeting in a few minutes so I'm going to head back. Good luck with that."

Trevor: "Thanks."

***

Situations like these are difficult when you don't agree with how the other person is seeing things. In Jacob's case, he likes Steven and believes he is deserving of the promotion. However, he also wants to preserve his relationship with Trevor. In truth, it probably isn't necessary for Jacob to share his opinion on the matter; it would likely be easier for him to simply listen, validate, and leave it at that. But his doing so here provides a useful example of how sharing a diverging opinion might be received, and how to handle it.

Notice how Jacob first asks a few questions to narrow down *why* Trevor doesn't like Steven. This helps him better understand the situation and where Trevor's perceptions are coming from, while also giving him something concrete to validate.

Next, he's careful to not immediately challenge Trevor's assumptions and instead chooses to validate the frustration. After acknowledging the difficulty of Trevor's circumstance, he asks permission to share his opinion.

Jacob validates Trevor *again*, then shares his own perspective. Notice how he avoids using "but" in his feedback. Had he said, "That's tough, *but* I've been very impressed with Steven's work," he would have negated the validating statement altogether and Trevor would have been more likely to get defensive.

Trevor does get defensive when he says, "I work *just* as hard," so notice again how Jacob goes back to validating and leaves it at that. In this instance (as Jacob is not Trevor's manager) it was probably wise to leave it there.

If Jacob were his manager, he would have the responsibility to give Trevor constructive feedback. In that case, he might choose to validate the fact that Trevor does work hard, and then help him understand that he's not working on the most important tasks, isn't delivering the quality expected, etc.

RWS #2: HIGH SCHOOL DRAMA

Sydney is a sixteen-year-old high school student complaining to her mom, Karen, about high school drama.

Sydney: "Ugh! I freakin' *hate* high school."

Karen: "What's going on?" **(L)**

Sydney: "I just found out that Hillary has been talking behind my back to Rachel and everyone else about me and telling them that I always steal all the guys she's interested in! And now I feel like they all hate me and they don't invite me to anything anymore."

Karen: "What? Why would she do that?" **(MV, L)**

Sydney: "I don't know! She's obviously interested in Zach, but Zach asked *me* out to the game this weekend. I didn't even *try* to get him. I wasn't even flirting with him!"

Karen: "Ah, so you think she's jealous?" **(L)**

Sydney: "Yeah! She totally is."

Karen: "And that's *got* to be frustrating to feel like all your friends are siding with her, without even giving you a chance to explain." **(V)**

Sydney: "Yeah, seriously."

Karen: "What are you going to do?" **(L)**

Sydney: "I don't know . . . I tried talking to Steph about it and she just looked at me like, *oh right, that's nice.* She didn't even listen."

Karen: "Ugh, that's rough. She didn't even listen?" **(V, L)**

Sydney: "No!"

Karen: "Wow, that *is* frustrating." **(V)**

(Karen pauses for a few moments to see if Sydney wants to share more.)

Karen: "I actually have a few ideas on how you could handle this. Would you like my opinion?" **(AP)**

Sydney: "Sure."

(Karen gives her feedback.)

Karen: "I'm sorry you're having to deal with this right now; the social scene in high school can be rough. If you ever want to talk more about it, or just vent, I'm all ears." **(VA)**

Sydney: "Thanks. I appreciate it."

***

In Karen's brief exchange with her daughter, she offers a nice mix of listening and validation. Notice how she paused for a few moments before asking permission to give feedback. While every situation is unique, pausing like this helps ensure you don't jump in with feedback too quickly. Even if you ask permission to share, you want to be sure you've given the other person a chance to get everything off their chest.

After you validate and pause for a moment, the other person will likely respond in one of two ways:

1. Soak up the validation and continue sharing (e.g. "EXACTLY! And *then* she said . . .")
2. Accept the validation and then pause (e.g. "Exactly.")

If the person continues to share, then continue to listen and give micro validation. If they accept the validation and then pause, you're in a good position to ask if they'd like feedback.

RWS #3: A FRIEND GOING THROUGH A DIVORCE

Lindsey and Kate are close friends.

Lindsey: "Hey Kate! How's it going?"

Kate: "Honestly, not well."

Lindsey: "Really? What's up?" **(L)**

Kate: "John just asked me for a divorce."

Lindsey: "Oh my gosh. Are you serious? Kate, I'm so sorry. [pause] When did this happen?" **(MV, L)**

Kate: "Last night."

Lindsey: "Did you know this was coming? Have you guys been having problems?" **(L)**

Kate: "Kind of. I don't know—I didn't really think *this* would happen. We've grown pretty distant over the past six months or so, but I guess I just thought that was normal. He just told me he's been seeing someone else."

Lindsey: "Are you kidding me? Ah, Kate . . . I am *so sorry.*" **(MV)**

(Lindsey pauses for a moment to see if Kate wants to share more).

Lindsey: "How are you feeling right now? It was just last night that he told you?"**(L)**

Kate: "Yeah. To be honest I'm pretty numb. I don't even really want to think about it right now."

Lindsey: "I don't blame you. I can't even imagine." **(V)**

Kate: "Yeah."

(There's a slight pause in the conversation and it becomes apparent that Kate doesn't want to talk much more about it.)

Lindsey: "Well hey, I'm here for you. I appreciate you letting me know—that's an incredibly heavy load to carry. I honestly can't even imagine. If you *ever* want to talk, know that I'm always willing to listen." **(VA)**

***

Notice how, instead of avoiding the topic and being worried about opening the wound with Kate, Lindsey asks a couple questions to better understand the situation.

Kate doesn't appear to be connected with her emotions right off the bat, so Lindsey asks how she is feeling. Even though Kate isn't able to pinpoint specific emotions, Lindsey still does her best to validate how difficult the situation must be.

There is certainly no room for feedback here, and it quickly becomes apparent that Kate doesn't want to talk much more, so Lindsey thanks her, validates her one more time, and leaves her with an open invitation to talk in the future.

RWS #4: GETTING A NEW JOB

Tyler and Alex are acquaintances. They know each other through a mutual friend and see each other every week or two.

Alex: "Tyler! It's been a while. How've you been?"

Tyler: "Great! Life is pretty good right now."

Alex: "Good to hear. How's work?" **(L)**

Tyler: "Fantastic actually—I just accepted a job at a new company!"

Alex: "Serious? Congratulations!" **(MV)**

Tyler: "Thank you!"

Alex: "What's the new position?" **(L)**

Tyler: "Customer Service Manager."

Alex: "Nice! You were on the customer service team at your last job, right? What's different about this new job?" **(MV, L)**

Tyler: "Well, before I was just taking calls every day (and getting yelled at) but now I'll be managing a team, training new hires, and working with upper management to improve the whole system. I'm pretty excited."

Alex: "I bet you'll be happy to get off the phones?" **(MV, L)**

Tyler: "Oh, you have no idea."

Alex: "I'm sure. People can be brutal over the phone. Having to deal with angry people every day has to take a toll." **(V)**

Tyler: "It does. I'm sure I'll still have to deal with the occasional angry customer, but far less often than I used to."

Alex: "Ah, that's so great." **(V)**

Tyler: "Yeah, I'm pretty excited!"

Alex: "Well seriously, congratulations, Tyler. When do you start the new position?" **(VA, L)**

Tyler: "Monday."

Alex: "You'll have to let me know how it goes!"

Tyler: "Thank you, I will."

***

In this exchange, Alex validated his friend in several casual, yet effective, ways. When Tyler shared the news of his new job, Alex saw an opportunity to validate the feelings of excitement and pride. By matching Tyler's energy and excitement, he showed that he was connected and appreciated the good news. He also used the "Guessing/Asking" technique to validate the difficulty of Tyler's old position—specifically the stress associated with working with angry customers.

This exchange was brief and casual, yet Alex's genuine interest in and positive response to Tyler's good news was almost certainly energizing. Chances are good that Tyler walked away with renewed excitement, as well as greater appreciation for Alex.

RWS #5: SPOUSE'S STRESSFUL DAY WITH KIDS

Kelli is a stay-at-home mom raising three young children. Mark comes home from work to find her notably frazzled.

Mark: "Hey, honey, how's your day been?"

Kelli: "Hectic."

Mark: "Really? What's up?" **(L)**

Kelli: "I just need a break."

Mark: "Kids not behaving?" **(L)**

Kelli: "No. But it's not just that. Trying to manage carpool, homework, soccer, making lunch, and keeping the house clean—all while trying to keep everyone alive? I'm not cut out for this."

Mark: "You do an *insane* amount of work every day. Trying to juggle all that would take a toll on anybody." **(V)**

Kelli: "If I can just get through today I'm sure I'll be fine."

Mark: "What more do you have to do?" **(L)**

Kelli: "I told Lex I'd read with her and then I need to finish the laundry."

Mark: "You've done more today than most people do in a week. We're both exhausted. How about I fold the laundry while you read to Lexi and we can both relax after that?" **(V)**

Kelli: "That sounds great. Thank you."

***

This exchange between Mark and Kelli is pretty straightforward, not requiring much beyond basic listening and validation. Notice how Mark asks a couple questions to encourage his wife to open up, then responds with a simple validating statement. From there, his empathy and love for his wife leads him to offer some relief from the stressful demands of the day as they both wind down for the evening.

RWS #6: BEING ACCUSED OF POOR SERVICE

Catherine is a receptionist at a service desk for a car dealership. A customer approaches her, angry at the fact that he's been waiting far longer than he expected and his car has still not been fixed.

> **Customer:** "This is ridiculous. I've been waiting here for nearly *two hours* now—way longer than the thirty minutes you promised—and you guys *still* haven't fixed my car! What the hell is going on?"

> **Catherine:** "I'm sorry, sir, I know this is frustrating. It has taken *far* longer than we told you. I am trying to get ahold of the mechanics to get more information for you on what's going on." **(V)**

> **Customer:** "This is the worst service I've ever had. This is a joke."

> **Catherine:** "I hear you. I'd be just as frustrated. I'm sure this has cut into other plans you've had or stopped you from getting to places you needed to be. If it would help, I can arrange for our shuttle service to take you wherever you need to go and pick you up when your car is ready, free of charge. I will also give you a call as soon as I get more information." **(V)**

> **Customer:** "No, I already missed my meetings. I want to talk to one of the mechanics."

> **Catherine:** "Absolutely. Someone will be right out to speak with you. Again, I do apologize. We do our best to give accurate estimates but obviously messed up

this time around. We will do what we can to make it right."

***

Dealing with angry customers is never a fun situation. In this example, Catherine does a nice job of validating the customer's frustration and doing what she can to make amends for the incorrect time estimate.

While she isn't able to get his car fixed any quicker, she is able to calm him down. She develops empathy for the man, realizing that he may now be late to a meeting, unable to run other errands, etc., which ultimately leads to more genuine and powerful validation.

Had Catherine become defensive, the situation would likely have escalated. Unfortunately, I see situations like this far too often. They go a little something like this:

Catherine: "I'm sorry, but that's just what I've been told. They're working as quickly as they can."

Customer: "This is ridiculous. You told me it would take thirty minutes!"

Catherine: "I know, but there's nothing I can do about it now. Please continue to be patient and I'll let you know as soon as I hear back."

Customer: "Be patient?! I've been patient for nearly *two hours!*"

Catherine: "Sir, calm down. I'll go talk to them and see if there's anything more they can do."

Customer: "Calm down? You're not the one whose been waiting for brake pad replacements for two hours!"

And so on. Can you spot Catherine's invalidating comments? They're everywhere. While she certainly means well, her efforts only serve to aggravate the situation. A simple shift into understanding and validating can make a night-and-day difference.

RWS #7: COMFORTING A YOUNG CHILD

Caden is four years old and is throwing a tantrum after realizing his mother has left for an evening out with her friends. Jim, his father, tries to comfort him.

Caden: "Where's mommy?!"

Jim: "She's gone out for a bit to play with her friends."

Caden: "I want to go!"

Jim: "Sorry, Caden. We can't go with mommy tonight. I'm here though; we can go play with your toys downstairs!"

Caden: "NO, daddy, I want *mommy!*"

Jim: "I know, Caden. It's sad when she leaves, isn't it?" **(L, V)**

Caden: (folding his arms and forcing a pouty face) "Yeah . . ."

Jim: "I miss her too. She's so kind and loving and is so great at reading stories, isn't she?" **(V, L)**

Caden: (still sniffling a little, but notably calmer) "Yeah."

Jim: "When she comes back, she promised to come tuck you in and read you a story. How does that sound?"

Caden: "Good."

Jim: "That will be fun. While we wait, we can make macaroni and cheese. Do you want to do that?"

Caden: "Okay . . ."

***

In the example above, Jim first tries to deflect or ignore Caden's visible disappointment by reminding him that *he* is still around. This quickly escalates Caden's emotions, leading to a more emphatic, "NO, daddy, I want *mommy!*"

As adults, we often try reasoning with young children when they're behaving irrationally. We might be thinking, "*Come on, kid*—she'll only be gone for two hours!" Yet, as any parent (or anyone who has babysat young children) can attest, these types of responses rarely help. Emotions are strong, unruly creatures, and to young children who haven't yet learned what they are and how to handle them, they can be quite frightening.

Once Jim recognizes that Caden needs validation, he shifts gears. As he validates Caden's sadness he is able to help him calm down. As Caden realizes that his dad understands what he's feeling and isn't judging him for it, he lowers his stubborn four-year-old walls and is able to accept the fact that his mom will be back later that evening.

FINAL THOUGHTS

"If you want to make a difference in someone's life, you don't need to be gorgeous, rich, famous, brilliant, or perfect. You just have to care."

– Karen Salmansohn

At this point, you should have a solid understanding of validation—what it is, why it's valuable, and how to offer it. We've discussed the whats and whys, walked through the Four-Step Method, and explored a handful of real-world examples to see the method in action. In this final chapter, we'll discuss a few final tips and recommendations for getting the most out of this powerful skill.

WHAT TO DO WHEN *YOU* NEED VALIDATION

With your increased understanding of validation, you are now much more likely to recognize when you yourself are seeking it. In these situations, it's often best to just ask for it directly.

I hit a point a few months ago where the stresses of work and life were weighing heavily on me. I decided to take a day off to catch up on things, take some me time, and get centered again.

After running a few errands, I stopped by a new barbershop, which my brother had told me about. The prices were more than double what I was used to spending on a haircut, but I figured it was worth trying something new.

After explaining to the barber what I was looking for, he quickly proceeded to do nothing of the sort. I watched a much larger chunk of my hair fall to the floor than I expected, and my heart sunk. You can't exactly uncut hair, so I reluctantly decided that my best option at that point was to let him finish and hope for the best.

As he wrapped up and spun me around to face the mirror, his face beamed with pride. I, on the other hand, was less than enthused. It wasn't necessarily a *bad* haircut, but it was certainly not what I had asked for and no longer allowed me to style it in the way that I liked.

I left the barbershop feeling very self-conscious. My mind shot ahead to the date I had that night, to what my coworkers would say the next day at work, and to whether or not there was something I could do to fix it.

After sinking further into shame about the fact that I was letting something as insignificant as a haircut completely ruin my day, I tried to bury it. "It's not a big deal," I said to myself. "Most people won't even notice." But then I would catch my reflection in the rearview mirror and my *real* thoughts would resurface: "Ugh, this does *not* look good." At this point I realized that I needed validation around my frustration and fear if I was going to let it go anytime soon.

I called a mentor of mine and told him I needed some validation and help getting out of my head. I explained the situation and how I felt stupid for letting it ruin my day.

"That's so frustrating, isn't it?" he said. "It's hard enough that you don't like it, but then you'll go to work tomorrow and people will be like, 'Whoa, what happened to your hair?'"

Those two comments—particularly the second one—immediately took a huge chunk out of my fear. As we talked, he never once tried to disregard my feelings. He never said anything like "I'm sure it's not *that* bad" or "People honestly won't even notice."

He told me that he too used to get self-conscious about his hair ("used to" because he's now bald) and that he could relate. After several genuine, validating remarks, I felt *world's* better and asked him for advice on how to get out of my head and move on. Sure enough, after just a few minutes of talking, I was able to move on with my day and let go of the embarrassment and fear I'd had around what others might think.

When you need validation, ask for it specifically. It's obviously best to talk with someone who already knows how to validate, but if the person you talk to doesn't, you can still point them in the right direction. For example, you might say:

> "Hey I'm feeling stressed right now and need some validation. Can I vent for a minute? I don't want feedback or any suggestions for fixing it. I'd just like you to hear me out and help me not feel crazy."

I had an opportunity to practice this just the other day when I started venting to a couple people in my family. They began to give advice and counsel and I found myself becoming irritated and defensive. I had literally *just* asked for their thoughts on the matter, then immediately went on the defensive against everything they were saying. It took me a few minutes to snap out of my own drama, but as I got curious about my defensiveness, I realized that I really just needed validation. I had already found a solution to the problem; I just wanted someone to appreciate the difficulty of the situation. I shared that with my family and they immediately stopped with the advice. Sure enough, with a little validation, I was able to let it go and felt significantly better.

LEARN TO VALIDATE YOURSELF

In addition to seeking validation from others, it's important to learn to validate *yourself.* We are often our own worst critics, judging ourselves in ways we never would another individual. Practicing self-compassion and learning to validate ourselves is a critical part of developing strong emotional health and happiness.

Like with validating others, self-validation can be used for both positive and negative experiences. This means you're allowed to feel pride and excitement when you do something well, and sadness or regret when things don't turn out the way you had hoped.

More often than not, we invalidate our emotions in an effort to avoid uncomfortable feelings such as fear, anger, or sadness. In the case of my bad haircut, I kept telling myself things like "it's not that big of a deal," "it'll grow back," or "no one will even notice."

You will recognize by now that these are invalidating statements and rarely help the situation. The "just get over it" or "don't get too excited" type responses weigh on us just as much as they would anyone else, yet are often difficult to catch in our own internal dialogue. Instead of dismissing or judging your own emotions, practice validating yourself in the same way you would a close friend. For example, you might say to yourself:

- "That's some quality work right there! I nailed it."
- "You know what? It makes perfect sense that I'm frustrated. I put a lot of time and effort into cooking this meal with the expectation that my husband and I could enjoy a nice evening together."
- "I actually have a lot on my plate right now—it makes total sense that I'm overwhelmed. I think anybody in my situation would feel the same way. It's probably worth taking a step back and slowing down."

Ignoring, dismissing, or suppressing your emotions doesn't get rid of them; it buries them. It tucks them away to fester and arise again at a later time. When you recognize and validate your emotions instead, you strip away the judgment—the "I'm bad," "this is wrong," or "I shouldn't" responses—and allow your experiences to flow through you. It helps you quell the inner critic and live a more present and enjoyable life.

WATCH YOUR EXPECTATIONS

As you begin to see firsthand the power validation has to put people at ease, help them out of a dark place, or compound their excitement and energy, you'll want to validate everyone you talk to. (And, honestly, there's no reason not to!)

Yet, as powerful as validation is, there will still be times when it doesn't "work." Even if you follow all the steps and genuinely want to connect with someone, they may choose not to be receptive. You can always validate someone, but you can't always guarantee that they'll accept your validation.

Several years ago, a friend of mine was chatting with one of his classmates. She was noticeably frustrated and began complaining about several problems she was facing. My friend listened, validated, and held off from giving advice while she talked through it. She vented for several minutes as he listened, empathized, and validated. Now, expecting to see relief in her eyes and a smile return to her face, my friend was surprised to hear her go right back to the beginning and start complaining all over again.

"It wasn't working!" he later told me. It didn't seem to matter what he said or how much he listened; she was deep in her own drama and refused to let it go. Having expected to "make everything better," my friend left feeling confused and down on himself. "I don't get it," he said to me, the frustration audible in his voice. "What did I do wrong?"

As he walked me through their conversation, I couldn't identify anything he'd done "wrong." While other factors could have been at play, it seemed that his friend simply wasn't in a place to accept the validation.

When I was in the early stages of writing this book, I met up with my family for dinner at a local restaurant. My father was visibly stressed from work, and I could see him fighting to keep his attention on the present moment. I asked him how his day had gone. "Okay," he replied. "Just okay?" I asked, inviting him to elaborate. "Yeah," came the response. "I spent far more time on a project today than I would have liked to."

I don't like seeing my father stressed and I very much wanted to try to help him feel better. We were in a loud, busy restaurant, however, and I could tell he wasn't in the mood to talk about it. He was notably and understandably burned out from a long day, and I decided to just let it be.

Whether the setting simply isn't right or the other person isn't willing to let go of their drama, don't get down on yourself when validating doesn't work out the way you'd hoped. There will always be other opportunities and trying to "force-validate" someone may only add to their frustration.

FINAL THOUGHTS: SUMMARY

Ask for validation when you need it. When you need validation, ask for it specifically rather than hoping others figure it out. If the person you're talking with isn't familiar with validation, fill them in on the basics and be specific about what you are and aren't looking for.

Learn to validate yourself. Resist the temptation to minimize or ignore your own emotions and focus instead on acknowledging and accepting them. Practicing self-compassion and learning to validate *yourself* is a critical part of developing strong emotional health and happiness.

Watch your expectations. Even if you follow all the steps and genuinely want to connect with someone, they may choose to not be receptive. You can always validate someone, but you can't always guarantee that they'll accept it or react in the way you'd hoped they would.

AFTERWORD

I hope you've found this book interesting, insightful, and helpful. Over the course of writing it, I've used the Four-Step Method in literally thousands of conversations. I've paid close attention to each of these, taking note of how they played out, then revisiting and refining the principles and techniques to ensure they were as practical, applicable, and effective as possible. Yet with that said, every person and situation is different, and mastery of the skill can only come from trial and error. I've been working on developing this skill for years now and still catch myself invalidating, offering unsolicited advice, and the like. When you catch yourself doing these things, don't sweat it. Just notice how it plays out. Ask yourself how you could have handled the situation differently and work on catching yourself sooner the next time.

If validating feels forced or awkward, experiment with different approaches, phrases, etc. until you find something that feels right to you. You can (and ought to) tailor the Four-Step Method to fit your own personality and interactions. With practice, you'll figure out how to effortlessly apply the steps in a natural, genuine way.

As you try it out, I would love to hear from you. Which principles have had the biggest impact? What successes have you seen? What advice would you give to others who are looking to improve their listening and validating skills? Shoot me an email at michael@ihearyoubook.com and let me know.

Finally, if these principles have made a positive impact in your life, please consider leaving a review on Amazon.com and/or passing a copy of the book along to a friend or family member. As powerful as these principles are, I am still amazed at how few people know about them. When you and others in your circle of influence know how to validate, everyone benefits. You are better able to show appreciation and support to those you love, and they, in turn, are able to offer the same.

It is my sincere hope that these principles and practices benefit your life as much as they have mine. Few experiences are more fulfilling than feeling truly, deeply, and sincerely connected to another human being. Few connections are more joyous than genuinely sharing in another person's excitement and good fortune. And few conversations are more rewarding than realizing you were there for someone during a time of need.

Remember: everyone you meet is afraid of something, loves something, and has lost something. Remember that we are all looking for love, appreciation, and connection. And remember that, regardless of age, gender, background, or ethnicity, being listened to—and heard—is one of the greatest desires of the human heart.

***

ENDNOTES

[1] Gottman, John. *The Relationship Cure: A 5 Step Guide to Strengthening Your Marriage, Family, and Friendships.* Reprint Ed., Harmony, 2002.

[2] Shenk, Chad E., and Alan E. Fruzzetti. "The Impact of Validating and Invalidating Responses on Emotional Reactivity." *Journal of Social and Clinical Psychology*, Vol. 30, No. 2, 2011, pp. 163-183.

[3] Gable, Shelly L., et all. "What Do You Do When Things Go Right? The Intrapersonal and Interpersonal Benefits of Sharing Positive Events." *Journal of Personality and Social Psychology*, Vol. 87, No. 2, 2004, pp. 228-245.

[4] "RSA Replay - The Power of Vulnerability." *YouTube*, uploaded by The RSA, July 4, 2013. https://www.youtube.com/watch?v=QMzBv35HbLk

[5] Billikopf, Gregorio. "Empathic Listening: Listening First Aid." *Meditate.com*, October, 2005. https://www.mediate.com/articles/encinaG3.cfm

[6] Cabane, Olivia Fox. *The Charisma Myth: How Anyone Can Master the Art and Science of Personal Magnetism.* 2/24/13 ed., Portfolio, 2013.

[7] Misra, Shalini et all. "The iPhone Effect: The Quality of In-Person Social Interactions in the Presence of Mobile Devices." *EDRA*, Vol. 48, Issue 2, 2014, pp. 275-298.

[8] Mehrabian, Albert, and Morton Weiner. "Decoding of Inconsistent Communications." *Journal of Personality and Social Psychology*, Vol. 6, Issue 1, 1967, pp. 109-114; Mehrabian, Albert, and Ferris, S.R. "Inference of Attitudes from Nonverbal Communication in Two Channels." *Journal of Consulting Psychology*, Vol. 31, Issue 3, 1967, pp. 48-258.

ABOUT THE AUTHOR

Michael S. Sorensen is a marketing executive by day and an avid reader, researcher, and personal development junkie by night. Obsessed with finding the best principles and practices for living a rich, fulfilling, and connected life, he seeks out and experiments with new and interesting ideas to discover what actually *works*. Having benefited from years of mentoring from coaches, counselors, and executives (and the wisdom of countless self-help books), he's set out to share his explorations, insights, and discoveries with others.